kitchen

Decorating Ideas & Projects

Better Homes and Gardens® Books
Des Moines, Iowa

Better Homes and Gardens® Books
An imprint of Meredith® Books

Kitchen Decorating Ideas
Editor: Linda Hallam
Art Director: Jerry J. Rank
Contributing Editors: Mary Baskin, Lynn McBride, Andrea Caughey, Nancy Ingram
Copy Chief: Catherine Hamrick
Copy and Production Editor: Terri Fredrickson
Book Production Managers: Pam Kvitne, Marjorie J. Schenkelberg
Contributing Copy Editor: Angela Renkoski
Contributing Proofreaders: Susan Sanfrey, Ann Marie Sapienza, Elizabeth White
Contributing Photographers: Jenifer Jordan, Cheryl Dalton, Ed Gohlich, Bill Rothschild
Indexer: Kathleen Poole
Electronic Production Coordinator: Paula Forest
Editorial and Design Assistants: Kaye Chabot, Mary Lee Gavin, Karen Schirm

Meredith® Books
Editor in Chief: James D. Blume
Design Director: Matt Strelecki
Managing Editor: Gregory H. Kayko
Executive Shelter Editor: Denise L. Caringer

Director, Retail Sales and Marketing: Terry Unsworth
Director, Sales, Special Markets: Rita McMullen
Director, Sales, Premiums: Michael A. Peterson
Director, Sales, Retail: Tom Wierzbicki
Director, Sales, Home & Garden Centers: Ray Wolf
Director, Book Marketing: Brad Elmitt
Director, Operations: George A. Susral
Director, Production: Douglas M. Johnston

Vice President, General Manager: Jamie L. Martin

Better Homes and Gardens® Magazine
Editor in Chief: Jean LemMon
Executive Interior Design Editor: Sandra S. Soria

Meredith Publishing Group
President, Publishing Group: Christopher M. Little
Vice President, Consumer Marketing & Interactive Media: Hal Oringer

Meredith Corporation
Chairman and Chief Executive Officer: William T. Kerr

Chairman of the Executive Committee: E. T. Meredith III

Cover Photograph: William Stites

All of us at Better Homes and Gardens® Books are dedicated to providing you with information and ideas to enhance your home. We welcome your comments and suggestions. Write to us at: Better Homes and Gardens Books, Shelter Editorial Department, 1716 Locust St., Des Moines, IA 50309-3023.

If you would like to purchase any of our books, check wherever quality books are sold. Visit our website at bhg.com or bhgbooks.com.

TIE-BACK – MEASURING UP

Loop the tape measure loosely around the curtains at the desired height, holding the ends so that they meet. This will be the finished length of the tie-back.

1. This curtain looks good with a simple rope tie-back, either in a color to match the main fabric of the curtain or the contrasting top band.

2. If you want to make a more dramatic tie-back, cut a rectangle of contrasting fabric to the required length and width, remembering to add seam allowances. You could shape the ends at this stage. For rounded ends, use a lid or saucer.

3. Cut out two pieces of fabric and one of interfacing. Place the interfacing on the wrong side of one piece of the fabric and iron in position. Place the fabric pieces right sides together and sew around the edges, leaving a gap of 2in (5cm) in the middle of one long edge. Turn through to the right side and slip-stitch the gap closed. Press.

4. Stitch braid all around the edges and sew a brass ring to either end to attach the tie-back to a hook on the wall.

stripey checked curtain

This unlined curtain can appear formal in a salon setting, as shown, or would look equally good in a country house. Either way, you can have fun attaching a multi-colored row of tassels to its edges. Try to find tassels which echo some of the colours in the checked curtain.

MATERIALS

◆ Curtains

◆ Tasseled fringing

◆ Rope and tassel tie-back

1. Tasseled fringing is usually made up of a braid from which a row of tassels hang. Sometimes the braid is decorative, but not always. You must decide whether to show the braid or not. To show it, pin the braid onto the right side, inner edge of the curtain from top to bottom. Turn in the ends to neaten. Machine-stitch along both long edges of the braid.

2. To hide the braid and show only the tassels, simply stitch the braid to the wrong side of the curtain, with one line of stitches nearest the curtain edge and another at the inside edge of the braid.

3. For a tie-back, you can use a length of rope, tied in a knot. Hand-stitch a tassel to each end to finish.

fancy footstool

This small item of furniture can become the focal decoration in a room with this easy-to-do treatment. The fabric cover is enhanced by the luscious fringing.

MATERIALS

◆ Fabric
◆ Tasseled fringing
◆ Rope and tassels

MEASURING UP

Measure from the base of the footstool, up and across the top, and down the other side. Do the same in the opposite direction. Cut a rectangle of fabric to these measurements plus 2½in (6cm) for hems.

1. Hem all four sides by turning ⅝in (1.5cm) to the wrong side. Press. Repeat, sew and press again.

2. Put the fabric rectangle over the footstool, wrong side up. Make sure that the fabric is centrally positioned and that the sides hang down evenly. Use pins to hold it in place around the top edges.

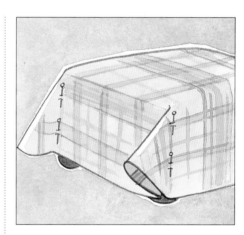

▲ **3. Stretch the fabric around the sides** of the stool until it is taut. Use pins to hold it in place. Pin the diagonal folds together at each of the corners. When satisfied, remove the fabric.

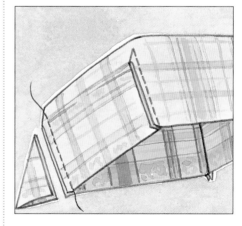

▲ **4. Sew along the diagonal folds of** fabric and then trim the seams. Replace the fabric over the footstool and adjust as necessary. Sew fringing around the lower edges of the fabric. Tie the tasseled rope into bows and stitch one to each top corner of the stool.

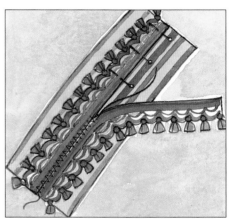

▲ **1. Stiffen the fabric with interfacing** and then fold it in half lengthwise. Mark the center with chalk on the right side. Pin a length of braid down the chalk line with the straight edge of the braid up against the line. When you reach the bottom edge, pleat or miter it neatly, and then pin the braid back up the other side of the chalk line. Ziz-zag stitch the two strips together down the center line. Sew the pleats or miters in place.

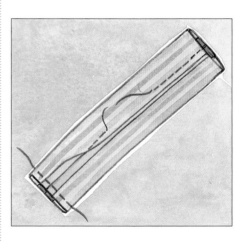

▲ **2. Fold the fabric in half lengthwise,** right side inward, and sew together using a ⅝in (1.5cm) seam allowance. Leave a 3in (8cm) gap in the center. Refold the fabric so that the seam and center chalk line are aligned. Sew across the ends. Turn the fabric right side out and slip-stitch the opening closed. Press.

bookmark

Enhance your library or study with this piece or give it to a bookworm friend as a present. Large and small versions can be made and any type of trimming added, depending on the look you are trying to achieve and what you have to hand. It's the perfect way to use up left-over scraps of trimmings from larger projects.

MATERIALS
◆ Fabric
◆ Tasseled braid
◆ Interfacing

MEASURING UP
Decide on the length and width required and double the width, adding seam allowances of ⅝in (1.5cm) all around.

picture hanger

This picture hanger is an attractive alternative to other ways of displaying your favorite photographs or prints. It is perfect for small portraits of family and friends, or a series of treasured images. Evocative of past times, it makes an ideal gift.

MATERIALS

◆ Fabric

◆ Tasseled braid

◆ Tassel

◆ Brass rings

MEASURING UP

Decide on the number and size of your pictures. This determines the length and width of your finished piece. Double the width and add seam allowances of ⅝in (1.5cm) all around.

1. Fold the fabric in half lengthwise and mark the center with chalk on the right side. Pin the tasseled braid along the chalk line, pleat or miter the corner, and then pin it back up the other side of the chalk line. The inside edges of the braid should butt up to the chalk line, or be positioned an equal distance away on either side. Sew around the inner and outer edges of the braid.

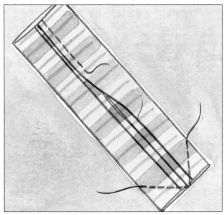

▲ **2. Fold the fabric in half lengthwise,** right side inward, and sew down its length, leaving a gap of 3in (7.5cm) in the center. Refold the fabric so that the center chalk line and seam are aligned. Draw a V shape at both ends of the fabric, making sure that they are symmetrical. Sew along the V shape and trim away the excess fabric. Turn the fabric right side out and slip-stitch the gap closed. Sew a brass ring at the top point of the picture hanger on the wrong side of the fabric.

3. Hand-sew a tassel to the lower point of the picture hanger. Sew further brass rings down the center of the braiding from which to hang the pictures.

tartan screen

A screen is a useful, movable piece of furniture which can be used to provide privacy, to protect from light or heat, or simply to divide a room into two spaces. Attach the fabric to the frame with ties or cords or simply staple in place. The trimming possibilities are endless, but always simple to apply.

MATERIALS

◆ Screen frame

◆ Fabric

◆ Fringing and tassels

MEASURING UP

Measure the width of the screen frame and add 2in (5cm) to each side. Measure the length of the frame and add 3in (8cm) to both top and bottom for hems. Add extra length to allow the fabric to be folded over/under the supporting battens of the screen frame if stapling the fabric in place. Cut two pieces of fabric per screen section.

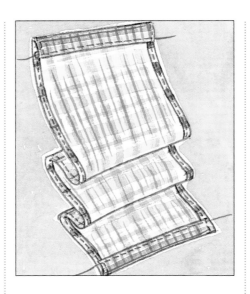

▲ 1. Hem the front and back pieces in the same way by turning the sides to the wrong side by 1in (2.5cm). Press. Repeat and sew. Turn the top and bottom hems to the wrong side by 1½in (4cm) and press. Repeat and sew. Press again.

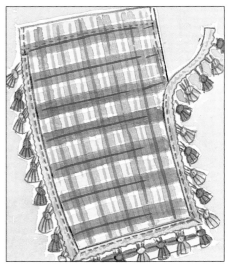

▲ 3. Remove the front piece of fabric from the frame. Pin fringing along the marked lines, mitering the corners. Sew in place. Tape the fabric in place to check that the fringing is correctly positioned. When satisfied, staple the fabric in place.

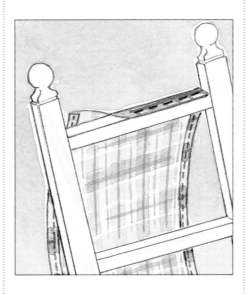

▲ 2. Place the top edge of the back piece on top of the upper supporting batten. Staple it in place. Make sure the fabric is pulled taut. Staple the bottom edge to the underside of the bottom batten. Tape the front piece in place and mark where the fringing is to be applied.

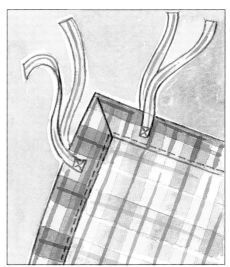

▲ 4. If you are using a frame without supporting wooden battens, you will not be able to staple the fabric directly to the frame. Instead, make fabric ties or use lengths of cord. Decide where best to position the ties and sew them in place before attaching the fringing.

knotted-corner pillows

These checked pillows are eye-catching on their own but are simply stunning with the addition of a twisted rope trimming. Just a little light hand-sewing will achieve this stylish look.

MATERIALS

◆ Pillow

◆ Twisted rope cord

▲ **1. To start, measure 1in (2.5cm) on either side of each corner and mark with a pin.** Start attaching the cord from the middle of one seam edge, pinning or basting it in place up to the corner mark.

▲ **2. Slip-stitch the straight run of cord firmly in place,** stopping at the pin. Make a loose, rounded knot in the cord at the corner point. Stitch the knot to hold its shape and to stop it from slipping. Return the cord to the straight edge at the second corner pin and continue slip-stitching to the next pin. Repeat the process for all of the corners.

▲ **3. Hide the ends of the cord by** opening up a small part of the pillow seam and slipping the ends through. Sew the seam closed again.

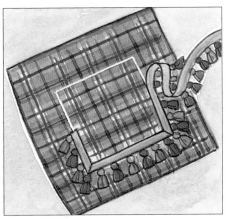

▲ **2. Draw the inner square on the** front piece of fabric with chalk, making sure that the lines are an equal distance in from all four edges. Pin the tasseled braid along the chalk line so that the tassels face outward. Miter the corners neatly. Sew along the inside and outside edges of the braid.

square pillow

Sometimes it is amusing to use two rows of trimming where one would do. The lavish use of decorative braid on this small pillow transforms it into one that looks rich and interesting.

MATERIALS
◆ Fabric
◆ Pillow form
◆ Tasseled braid

MEASURING UP

The front piece should be the size of the pillow form plus 1½in (3cm) all around for seam allowances. For the back piece, add a further 4in (10cm) to the depth and then cut it in half depthwise.

1. Take the two halves of the back piece and turn ⅝in (1.5cm) to the wrong side along the cut edge of each. Press. Turn the same amount again, sew and press. Overlap the hemmed sides by 2in (5cm). Baste together at the ends.

▲ **3. Lay the front and back pieces** together, right sides facing, and sew around the edges using a seam allowance of ⅝in (1.5cm). Turn right side out and press. Pin more braid around the side edges of the pillow so that the tassels fall evenly over the side seams. Miter the corners as before and sew the braid in place around both its inside and outside edges. Insert the pillow form.

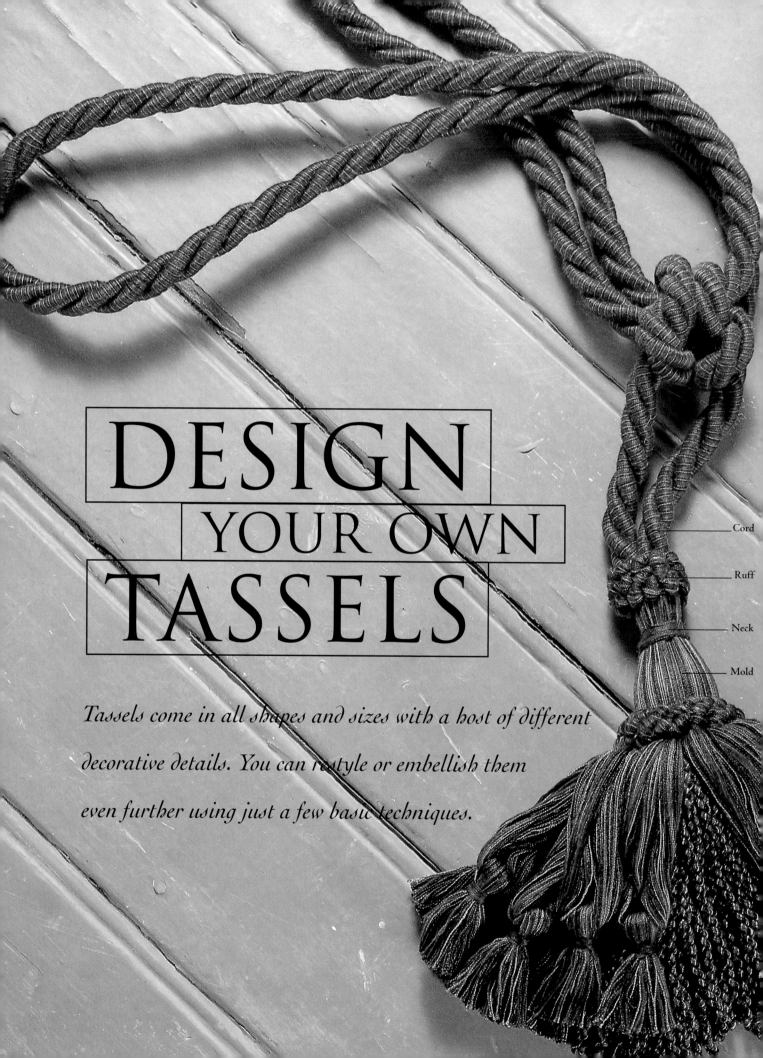

DESIGN
YOUR OWN
TASSELS

Cord

Ruff

Neck

Mold

Tassels come in all shapes and sizes with a host of different

decorative details. You can restyle or embellish them

even further using just a few basic techniques.

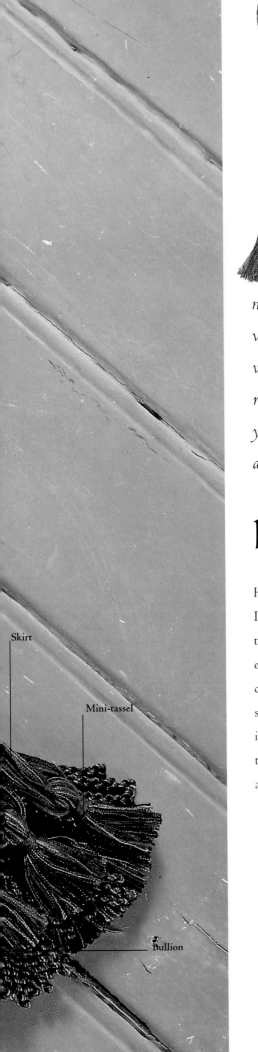

*T*here are a multitude of tassels available, but even so, you may not always be able to find something suitable. The tassels you find might not fit into your chosen design theme, or they could be too plain when what you really want is something unique and special. Tassels can also be very expensive, and often it is cheaper to dress up a simple tassel or to restyle one you already have. Customizing your tassels to coordinate with your room is really quite simple to do, and can easily be achieved without any special equipment.

basic techniques

Here are three simple techniques for dressing up your tassels. In the following projects, you will see examples of how they are used, but do not be afraid to experiment. All of these techniques can be used for each of the styles featured in this book; it is simply a case of choosing the right materials and colors and using your imagination!

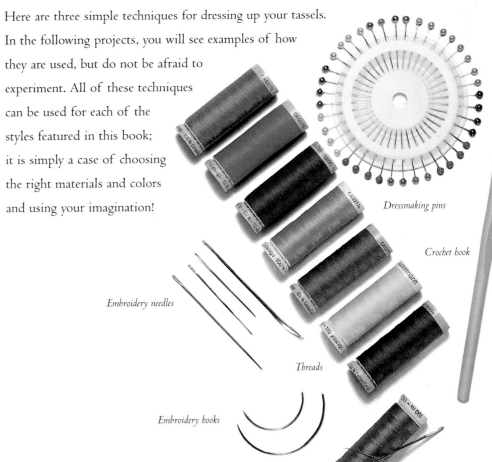

Skirt

Mini-tassel

Bullion

Dressmaking pins

Crochet hook

Embroidery needles

Threads

Embroidery hooks

braiding

Ribbons, yarns, threads and strips of fabric can be braided together and used to decorate tassels in many ways. The braids can be attached to the skirt of the tassel or around its neck. They can be looped to form rosettes and used to decorate the mold. The list is endless.

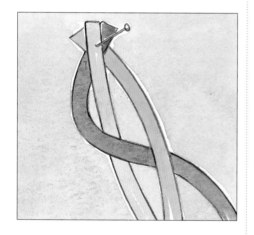

▲ **I. Fasten three ribbons together** at one end. Cross the left-hand ribbon over the middle ribbon, and then cross the right-hand ribbon over this one.

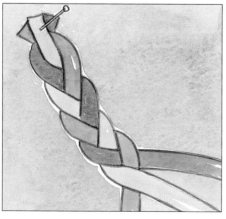

▲ **2. Repeat this step until the desired** length is reached, adjusting the tension as required. Secure the ends by wrapping.

wrapping

You can wrap almost any material around any part of a tassel. It is an effective form of decoration in itself, as well as a useful way to fasten other forms of decoration to a tassel. Wrapping is also used to finish off the ends of braids and bullions, etc, so that they do not unravel. The important thing is to keep the wraps neat and to position them strategically. In the following illustrations, some of the wraps are shown widely spaced. This is for clarity only, so that you can easily see what is happening underneath the wraps. Widely spaced wraps would not be secure and would look untidy.

I. If wrapping the tassel with a soft material, such as thread or knitting yarn, lay the end of the thread along the section of the tassel that you want to bind. Hold the thread firmly in place with your fingertip.

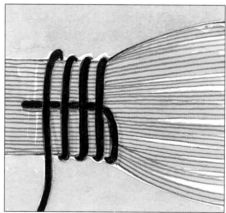

▲ **2. Begin wrapping the thread around** the tassel, trapping the end of the thread underneath the wraps. Take care to lay each successive wrap neatly next to the previous one. Keeping the thread taut at all times, continue wrapping until the desired width is reached.

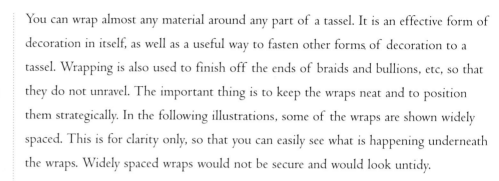

▲ **3. Use a needle to pull the remaining** end of the thread back under the wraps. Pull through until neat, and then cut off the excess thread.

4. If wrapping your tassel with a stiff material, such as seagrass, first cut a 20in (50cm) length of strong thread and keep nearby. Start wrapping the material around the tassel in exactly the same way as for a soft material.

bullions

One of the most effective ways to dress up the skirt of a tassel is to use bullions. These are made from one or more cords, which are twisted tightly and then looped in half so that both halves of the cord twist around each other. They are a good way to add a touch of luxury to a tassel that is made from plain materials.

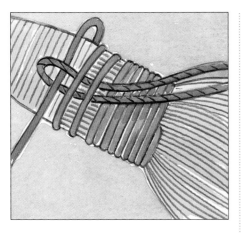

▲ **5. Continue wrapping until you are** near the desired finished width (around 6 wraps from this is best). Place the strong thread in a loop along the tassel, with the loop lying in the direction you are working. Continue wrapping around both the tassel and the loop of thread.

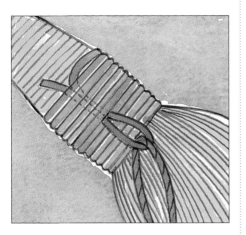

▲ **6. When the desired width is** reached, put the end of the wrapping material through the loop. Pull the ends of the looped thread so that the wrapping material is eased under the wraps. Pull all of the way through until neat, and then trim off any excess wrapping material.

▶ **1. For each** bullion, use cord or strands of thread that are at least double the required finished length. First, tie one end of the cord to something steady. A door handle is ideal. Tie the other end of the cord to the middle of a pencil.

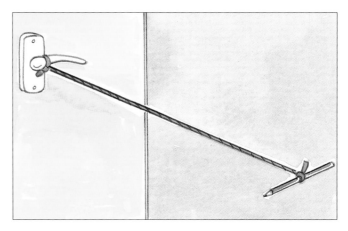

2. Rotate the pencil clockwise with one hand, until the cord is twisted tightly. Maintain tension on the cord while doing this by slipping it between the middle fingers of your other hand and pulling it straight outward from the door.

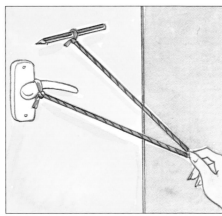

▲ **3. When finished, use the hand that** was rotating the pencil to hold the middle of the twisted cord between a finger and thumb. Maintain the tension at the pencil end with your other hand. Fold the cord in half, keeping it taut.

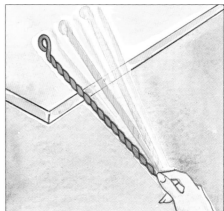

▲ **4. Holding both ends of the cord** between your finger and thumb, release the middle of the cord, allowing it to twist onto itself. Untie the ends from the door handle and pencil. Still holding the ends firmly, hit the edge of a table with the twisted cord to even out the twists. Secure the loose ends to stop the bullion from unwinding by wrapping.

ethnic tassel

This is a tassel that you can make entirely on your own. A long cord of pom-poms forms the skirt of the tassel, but you could use other types of decorative cord just as easily. Try to find one with a bold base color and be equally daring in your choice of yarns.

MATERIALS

◆ Wooden curtain ring

◆ Long strip of pom-pom cord

◆ Black knitting yarn

◆ Remnants of brightly colored knitting yarn (red, purple, turquoise, green and yellow are used here)

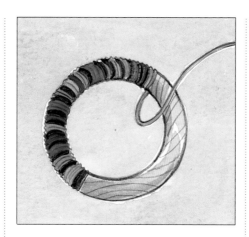

▲ **1. Wrap the entire wooden ring with** black yarn, interspersed with wraps of brightly colored yarn. Use the bright colors at random and allow the black to show through between each color section.

▲ **2. Tie the center of a single 28in** (70cm) strand of black yarn to the ring (it is shown in red here for clarity only). To make the hanging cord, measure a 24in (60cm) hank of black yarn containing 20 strands. Keeping the looped ends neat and the hank taut, pass the hank through the center of the ring. Fold the hank in half over the original single strand of yarn.

3. Keep the single strand of yarn in the center of the hank at all times so that the hanging cord of the tassel can be bunched up later to give a bobbled effect.

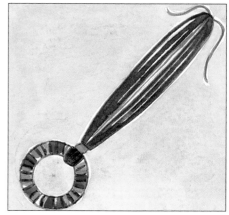

▲ **4. Wrap a piece of colored yarn** around the hank to secure it close to the ring. Remember to keep the original strand of yarn in the center. Hold the loops at the top of the hank in place by tying a short piece of yarn through them.

▲ **5. Wrap different colored yarns at** random around the cord at approximately 1in (2.5cm) intervals. Make the top wraps slightly smaller than the lower ones to give an illusion of weight to the ring. Leave 3in (7.5cm) of black yarn free at the top to form the hanging loop.

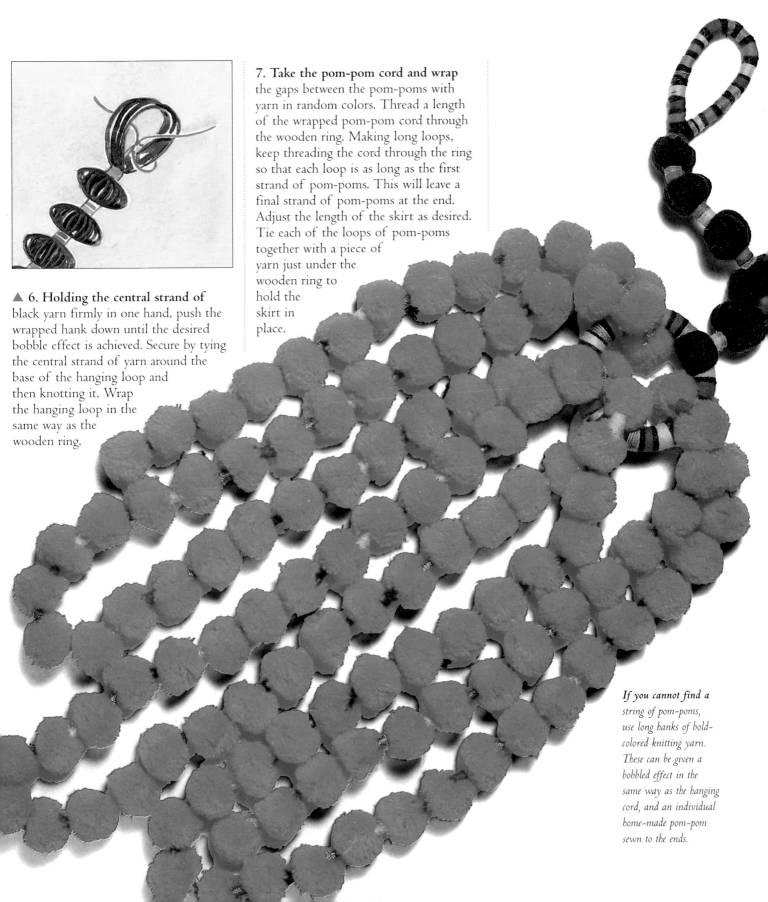

7. Take the pom-pom cord and wrap the gaps between the pom-poms with yarn in random colors. Thread a length of the wrapped pom-pom cord through the wooden ring. Making long loops, keep threading the cord through the ring so that each loop is as long as the first strand of pom-poms. This will leave a final strand of pom-poms at the end. Adjust the length of the skirt as desired. Tie each of the loops of pom-poms together with a piece of yarn just under the wooden ring to hold the skirt in place.

▲ **6. Holding the central strand of** black yarn firmly in one hand, push the wrapped hank down until the desired bobble effect is achieved. Secure by tying the central strand of yarn around the base of the hanging loop and then knotting it. Wrap the hanging loop in the same way as the wooden ring.

If you cannot find a string of pom-poms, use long hanks of bold-colored knitting yarn. These can be given a bobbled effect in the same way as the hanging cord, and an individual home-made pom-pom sewn to the ends.

classical tassel

This tassel treatment shows how to add a top layer of mini-tassels to an existing tassel skirt. The double-coin knots are the main decorative focus, and also echo the netting on the mold of the main tassel. The braiding around the skirt and mold provide the finishing touches.

A plain black tassel *would contrast too strongly with the pale whites and creams used in the classical section. Adding a few touches of white and gold provides just the right link.*

MATERIALS

◆ Round gold-and-white cord

◆ Flat gold cord

◆ Flat white cord

◆ White rayon thread

◆ Gold metallic sewing thread

◆ White sewing thread

◆ Black sewing thread

◆ Square of stiff cardboard
(the sides should be the required length of the mini-tassels)

◆ Pinboard or firm cushion

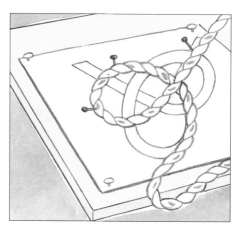

▲ **1. Take a photocopy of the double-coin knot template** on page 114. Pin it to a pinboard. Using the round gold-and-white cord and starting 1in (2.5cm) along from the end of the cord, lay it on top of the template, starting at point A and securing it to the board with pins. Follow the pattern of the template with the rest of the cord, copying the path exactly and passing under or over the previously positioned cord as required.

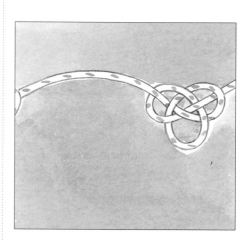

▲ **2. When complete, remove the knot** from the board and carefully adjust until it measures around ⅝in (2cm) square. Measure 2in (5cm) from the left-hand side of the knot along the remaining length of cord, and pin it to the board at point A. Make the next knot as before. Repeat until you have six knots.

3. Wind white rayon thread around the piece of cardboard 24 times. Hold the threads at the top of the cardboard and then cut the loops at the lower edge. Keep hold of the threads securely.

▲ **4. Pull the rayon threads** through the lower loop of one of the double-coin knots using a crochet hook, so that all the ends are level. Wrap the rayon threads with gold metallic thread, close to the double-coin knot, to secure. Repeat for all six knots.

The shininess of the cord and the rayon threads is extremely effective against the matte background of this tassel. However, it would look just as good on a shiny background so long as the color contrast was sufficient.

◄ 7. Braid together two lengths of flat gold cord with one length of flat white cord. Measure and cut the braid so that it fits around the tassel at the top of the skirt. Wrap each cut end immediately with gold thread to prevent fraying and unraveling. Position the braid around the tassel, covering the stitches holding the knotted cord in place. Butt the ends of the braid together, pin, and stitch neatly to the tassel using gold thread. Wrap a band of braid around the base and top of the mold in the same way.

▲ 5. Position six marker pins, evenly spaced, around the tassel at the top of the skirt. Attach the knotted cord, halfway between each of the knots, to the tassel at the marker pins. Cross the ends of the cord, making sure that the first and last knots are level with the rest. Trim the ends of the cord neatly above the pin. If the cord is likely to fray, you may need to wrap with white thread first. Using black thread, carefully stitch the cord to the tassel at the marker pins.

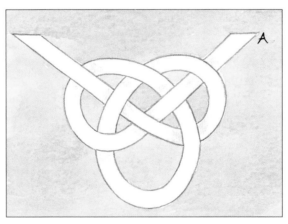

The double-coin
knot is easy to make,
but you may find it
easier to work from
an enlarged photocopy
of the template, left.

You may need to
adjust the quantity of
cord between knots so
that they fit around the
tassel but still hang to
the correct depth. You
may also want to add
more knots. Let the size
of the tassel dictate this.

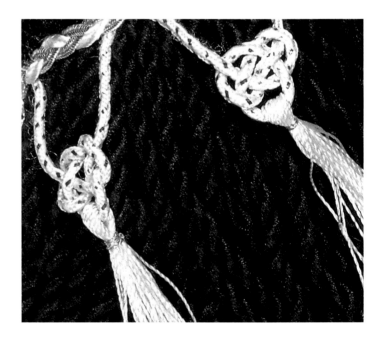

▲ 6. Trim the rayon tassels hanging from the decorative knots to the same length as the existing skirt of the tassel, taking care to cut only the white threads.

cool calicoes

Some tassels have skirts made up of mini-tassels, and their molds may be interesting shapes or perhaps decorated with fancy ruffs. These features can be emphasized simply by wrapping. Choose wrapping threads that coordinate with the colors of the fabrics in your design scheme.

MATERIALS

◆ Blue embroidery thread
◆ White embroidery thread

Small tassels, particularly ones with existing decorative detail such as mini-tassels around the skirt and wide ruffs, could look too fussy if you add too much extra decoration. Concentrate on emphasizing the existing detail instead.

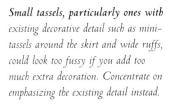

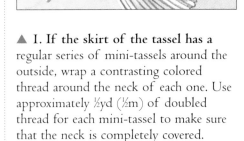

▲ **1. If the skirt of the tassel has a** regular series of mini-tassels around the outside, wrap a contrasting colored thread around the neck of each one. Use approximately ½yd (½m) of doubled thread for each mini-tassel to make sure that the neck is completely covered.

2. If the skirt is entirely made up of mini-tassels, first check that there are an even number of them around the outside circumference of the skirt. If there is an uneven number, carefully bring a tassel up from the row underneath using a crochet hook. Wrap alternate mini-tassels with a contrasting colored thread.

▲ **3. Wrap the mold and/or neck** with contrasting colored thread. Choose the points to wrap carefully. If there is already some decoration around the neck or mold of the tassel, such as a thick ruff, a single band of wraps will be sufficient. If the mold of the tassel is an interesting shape, consider highlighting this by strategically placing the wraps to emphasize the shape. Always keep the wrapping even and level.

french tassel

In your search for tassels, you will certainly discover many beautiful and unusual ones, and yet, however much you like them, they may not quite fit into your room scheme. Let this be your chance to try some unusual embellishments, such as these pretty "treble flowers."

Always look carefully at the tassel's existing features and then decide whether to complement or contrast with them, in shape, color and material. Here the colors and materials contrast, but the shapes of the decoration complement.

MATERIALS

◆ Flat, ornate braid

◆ Double gimp

◆ Metallic cord

◆ Madeira-gold sewing thread

◆ Invisible thread

◆ Glue

1. Mark the circumference of the tassel mold into quarters with pins top and bottom. Cut four lengths of ornate braid, each slightly longer than the mold. Glue the ends to prevent fraying. Center a length of braid on one of the quarter marker pin at the top of the tassel and carefully fit it up to the hanging cord. Stitch it in place with invisible thread. Pin the rest of the braid down the length of the mold and stitch in place. Trim the bottom to fit neatly behind the pompoms of the skirt and glue in place. Attach the remaining lengths of braid at the other quarter marks.

2. Repeat this process to sew a length of double gimp along either side of each strip of ornate braid. Then stitch metallic cord on either side of this, tidying the ends as before.

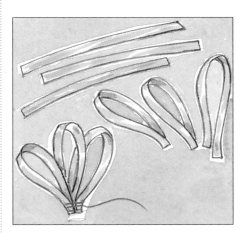

▲ **3. For each treble flower for the** skirt of the tasssel, cut three 2in (5cm) lengths of metallic cord. Glue the ends of the pieces of cord to prevent fraying, and then fold each one in half to form a loop. Bind all six loop ends together by wrapping with gold thread. Make more as required (27 are used here).

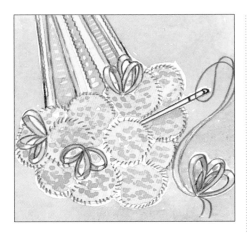

▲ **4. Stick a pin through the center of** each flower and push them in between the pom-poms. When the desired effect is achieved, remove the flowers one by one, place a dab of glue at the base of each and replace. Hold them in place with the pin until dry and then remove the pins. Alternatively, sew them in place.

5. Glue each end of a length of metallic cord to prevent it from fraying. Take a needle threaded with invisible thread, doubled and knotted, and sew a line of running stitches through the cord at 1in (2.5cm) intervals. Try to keep to one side of the cord. Pull the thread tight to make the cord loop up.

6. Wrap the looped ruff around the hanging cord at the top of the tassel, pulling evenly. Bind the invisible thread around the center of the ruff to hold it in place. Keeping the thread taut, stitch through the ruff several times to secure, and then cut the thread. Wrap the center of the ruff with gold thread so that the invisible thread is completely covered. Fasten off as before.

You will usually find that bold decoration, such as these ornate gold braids and loops, will look best against neutral colors. The trick is to find a tassel with an interesting shape to counter the boldness of the embellishment.

floral tassel

Neutral-colored tassels are always a good starting point, whatever your decorative scheme. If the material of the tassel is rough, satin ribbons and silk flowers will help to add shine and sparkle — and there are plenty of other motifs available as well as the roses used here.

MATERIALS
◆ Small peach silk roses
◆ Green knitting ribbon
◆ 4-ply knitting yarn, of a similar shade to the knitting ribbon
◆ Narrow peach ribbon
◆ Narrow green ribbon
◆ Toning sewing threads

▲ 1. Pin three roses, evenly spaced, around the neck of the tassel (or at the top of the mold if there is no neck). Pin five roses around the bottom of the mold, on the ruff if there is one. Stitch in place and remove the pins.

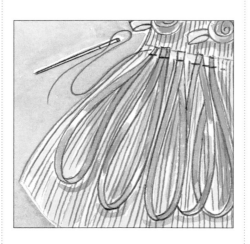

▲ 2. Make the ribbon skirt. Pin loops of ribbon evenly around the existing skirt, making sure the loops all hang to the same length. Alternate between the two colors of ribbon. Stitch the ribbon in place around the top of the skirt, close to the ruff. Remove the pins.

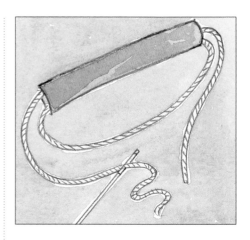

▲ 3. Make the four ruches of knitting ribbon to go above and below the rows of roses. You will need approximately four times the relevant circumference of the tassel, plus twice that amount of knitting yarn for each one. Thread a tapestry needle with the knitting yarn and thread this carefully through the knitting ribbon. Take the needle back around to the beginning and thread through again to form a loop.

▲ 4. Place the loop over the tassel and position as required. Pull the ends of the yarn tightly to ruche the ribbon until the ends meet. Maintaining tension, sew in the ends of the knitting yarn, concealing them under the ruched ribbon.

▲ **5. Make sure that the lowest ruche** of knitting ribbon covers the stitching of the ribbon skirt, sewing it in place with tiny stitches if necessary.

▲ **6. To finish, sew a peach** rose to the bottom of each of the loops of the peach ribbon skirt.

Soft pastel colors are ideal for floral tassels. However, the range of colors found in nature is myriad, so choose according to your tastes.

rustic tassel

While there are many rustic-style tassels available, you will find that they can often be rather dull. This is an example of how to dress up such a tassel with subtlety and natural charm. You will find seagrass and reindeer moss — and a wealth of other wonderful rustic materials — at most florists' stores.

MATERIALS

◆ Seagrass
    ◆ Reindeer moss
        ◆ Glue
            ◆ Toning sewing thread

Search for natural materials with different textures to add contrast to a monotone tassel.

▲ **I. Cut the seagrass into lengths** twice as long as the existing skirt of the tassel. Bend each length in half, and sew them around the top of the skirt using strong thread and a tapestry needle.

2. When the seagrass is secure, untwist each length up to the stitching. Trim the ends to the desired length.

▲ **3. Glue pieces of reindeer moss** around the mold of the tassel until it is completely covered. Use small, irregular-shaped pieces so that the textural effect is further enhanced. Wrap the top of the skirt four times with seagrass, making sure that the stitching is hidden.

medieval tassel

The rich colors and textiles that were used to adorn churches and palaces in medieval times provide the perfect inspiration to create a gloriously sumptuous tassel — and what better way than by adding a layer of shining bullions and rosettes highlighted with beads.

You should have no difficulty finding tassels made in rich colors and materials. However, do not worry if you cannot. Simply add a double- or treble-layer of shining bullions to the skirt, and more rosettes and/or beads to the mold, neck and ruffs. Let your imagination run riot!

MATERIALS

◆ Space-dyed knitting ribbon

◆ Gold knitting ribbon

◆ Black double-knitting yarn

◆ Gold beads

◆ Masking tape

◆ Vilene binding

◆ Toning sewing threads

▲ **1. First, make the ruched rosettes.** You need to make enough to surround the neck of the tassel completely. Cut a 10in (25cm) length of space-dyed knitting ribbon for each one. Feed doubled sewing thread carefully through the knitting ribbon using a tapestry needle. Take the needle back round to the beginning and thread through again to form a loop. Pull the ends of the thread until a rosette is formed. Leave a small space in the center of each one so that you can sew a gold bead in place.

▲ **2. Baste through the back of the** rosettes in a straight line with doubled sewing thread. Position them around the neck of the tassel, pull tight, and knot. Cut off the excess thread, and sew the ends into the back of the rosettes.

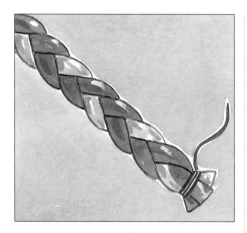

▲ **3. Make the eight spiral rosettes for** the top of the tassel skirt. Braid three lengths of space-dyed knitting ribbon together. Cut this into four equal lengths, binding the ends of each piece securely with toning thread. Repeat this process with two lengths of space-dyed and one length of gold knitting ribbon. You should experiment first with a single rosette to calculate how much braid to make and what size the spirals must be.

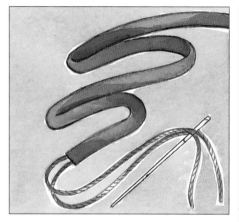

▲ **5. To make the bullion skirt, you** must first measure the length of the existing tassel skirt. Cut twelve lengths of space-dyed knitting ribbon to twice that measurement and twelve lengths of double-knitting yarn to four times the measurement. Fold each length of yarn in half. Use a tapestry needle to thread the doubled-over yarn through the lengths of ribbon, and then use these to make twelve bullions.

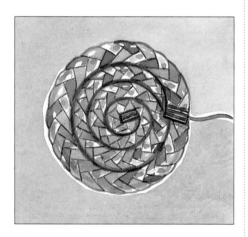

▲ **4. For each rosette, fasten a piece of** masking tape onto an ironing board, sticky side up. Form a length of braid into a spiral on the masking tape, leaving the bound ends on the top surface (this will be the back of the rosette). Iron a square of vilene onto the spiraled braid to secure (use a damp cloth on top of the vilene). Remove the masking tape and trim away the excess vilene. Sew a gold bead onto the center front of the rosette.

▲ **6. Cut twelve lengths of space-dyed** knitting ribbon, twelve lengths of gold knitting ribbon and twelve lengths of double-knitting yarn, all to twice the length of the existing tassel skirt. Thread the yarn through the lengths of space-dyed knitting ribbon. Twist a length of stuffed ribbon with a length of gold ribbon approximately 35 times to form a bullion. Repeat until you have made twelve of these.

The knitting ribbon used to make the bullions is given thickness by inserting knitting yarn. If you prefer, you can use round cord to make the bullions instead. Flat cord would be the easiest alternative for making the rosettes.

▲ **7. Check that all of the bullions are** the same length as the tassel skirt and adjust as necessary. Position four marker pins, evenly spaced, around the tassel at the join between the skirt and the mold. Sew three of the space-dyed bullions together, side by side, at their top edges. Attach them to the tassel at one of the marker pins. Repeat at the other three marker pins. Sew three of the gold bullions together and then sew to the tassel in between the others. Repeat until the bullion skirt is complete.

8. Sew the spiral rosettes on top of the bullion strands at the join of the mold and skirt, matching the two types.

tartan tassel

Tartan-ize your tassel with a ribbon skirt — a fun idea that is very simple to do. Go one step further by adding checks around the mold — this is even more effective if the mold has netting.

MATERIALS
◆ Tartan ribbon
◆ Narrow red ribbon
◆ Narrow orange ribbon
◆ Narrow blue ribbon
◆ Dark-green sewing thread

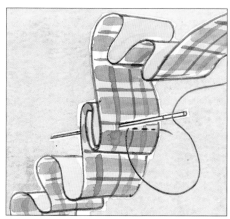

▲ **1. Take the tartan ribbon and join** both ends together to make a felled seam, as shown. Make sure that you keep the ribbon straight when doing this.

2. Using doubled sewing thread, sew a row of basting stitches along one edge of the ribbon. Put the ribbon around the top of the skirt of the tassel and gather the thread to secure it in place. Adjust to fit, and then knot securely.

▲ **3. Sew the underside of the gathered** ribbon to the tassel to hold it firmly in place. Make sure that the stitching is kept close to the ruff so that it is concealed.

▲ 4. **Cut three strips each of red,** orange and blue ribbon. Using a tapestry needle, thread each piece of ribbon in color sequence under the netting around the mold, leaving enough at each end to tuck in neatly later.

▲ 5. **Repeat this process, threading the** colored ribbons in the opposite direction so that the ribbons cross over and under each other alternately. Again, leave enough at each end to tuck in later.

▲ 6. **Using a tapestry needle, tuck each** piece of ribbon into the ruff at the top and bottom of the mold. Trim the length if necessary.

Try to match the colors in the ribbon skirt with those used around the mold. All of the colors must, of course, coordinate with that of the base tassel.

index

credits

Quarto would like to acknowledge and thank the following for providing pictures used in this book. Ace Photo Agency/Brian Green, page 8 (right); GP & J Baker, pages 59, 104 (Divertimenti range); Crowson Fabrics Ltd, page 51 (Ikatania range); Elizabeth Whiting Associates, pages 33, 53, 56, 58, 68, 89; BT Archive, pages 7 (below), 9 (below); Lara Grylls PR, page 35 (Monkwell Naturals range); Giulia Hetherington, page 9 (above); Nobilis-Fontan, pages 79 (Archang et Gouny), 98 (Lampas Broches); Osborne & Little, pages 19 & 21 (Nomad range), 90 (Abruzzo range);

All other photographs are the copyright of Quarto.

The following kindly loaned items for use in photography:
Early's of Witney, Oxfordshire (throw, page 16); John Edgson, Cirencester (curtain, page 27; ottoman, page 54; table cover, page 65; curtain, page 85; screen, page 103); Liberty's, London (tassel, page 106); the Pukka Palace, London (bed, page 29); Celestino Valenti Wireworks (corona, page 29)

Project Makers
Quarto would like to thank Elizabeth Valenti *for designing and making many of the soft furnishing projects used in this book, and also* Tessa Hadley *and* Jan Williams *for their assistance in the making of these projects.*

We would also like to thank Janet Oliver *and the students of* Kidderminster College, Hoo Road, Kidderminster, Worcestershire DY10 1LX, *for making the "design your own tassels" projects.*
Denise Craig *(classical and calico tassels)*
Victoria Floyd *(floral and rustic tassels)*
Faye Halstead *(medieval tassel)*
Niclola Parle *(tartan tassel)*
Nicky Taylor *(ethnic and French tassels)*

Quarto would particularly like to acknowledge and thank **Conso Products Company**, South Carolina, USA, who so kindly supplied all of the tassels and trimmings used in the projects made for this book. Conso produce an extremely wide range of tassels and trimmings, and welcome orders worldwide. Their company also incorporates British Trimmings and Wendy Cushing, both of which are based in the UK.

GP & J Baker
PO Box 30
West End Road
High Wycombe HP11 2QD
Tel: (UK) 01494 467467

British Trimmings
PO Box 46
Coronation Street
Stockport SK5 7PJ
Tel: (UK) 0161 480 6122

Celestino Valenti Wireworks
The Wire Workshop
Brewery Arts
Brewery Court
Cirencester
Gloucestershire GL7 1JH
Tel: (UK) 01285 642583

Conso Products Company
PO Box 326
513 N. Duncan Bypass
Union
South Carolina
SC 29379
Tel: (US) 800 845 2431

Crowson Fabrics Ltd
Crowson House
Bellbrook Park
Uckfield
East Sussex TN22 1QZ
Tel: (UK) 01825 761055

Wendy Cushing
7 Chelsea Harbour Design Centre
London SW10 0XE
Tel: (UK) 0171 351 5796

Early's of Witney
New Witney Mill
Witney
Oxfordshire
OX8 5EB
Tel: (UK) 01993 703131

John Edgson
Dyer Street
Cirencester
Gloucestershire GL7 1JH
Tel: (UK) 01285 640886

Just Fabrics
Burford Antiques Center
Cheltenham Road
Burford
Oxfordshire
OX18 4JA
Tel: (UK) 01993 823391

Monkwell Ltd
10–12 Wharfdale Road
Bournemouth
Dorset BH4 9BT
Tel: (UK) 01202 762456

Nobilis-Fontan
1 & 2 Cedar Studios
45 Glebe Place
London SW3 5JB
Tel: (UK) 0171 351 7878

Osborne & Little
49 Temperley Road
London SW12 8QE
Tel: (UK) 0181 675 8254

Pukka Palace
174 Tower Bridge Road
London SE1
Tel: (UK) 0171 234 0000

Whiteheads Fabrics Ltd
Dominion Way West
Southdownview Road
Worthing
West Sussex BN14 8NW
Tel: (UK) 01903 212222

contents

gettingstarted

Where do you spend most of your waking, at-home hours? Where do your family and guests **like to congregate?** The answer to both questions is most likely the kitchen—from the first cup of coffee in the morning to a glass of wine before dinner. **Enjoy your kitchen and welcome friends** by making it as attractive as it can be. As you'll see in this book, **kitchens of many different sizes, styles, and designs can be well-decorated,** inviting spaces. Begin with a plan and structure and then add your favorite colors, fabrics, furnishings, and accessories to make it your own space. **Start by determining your design goals.** If you are building a new house or remodeling your existing kitchen, take advantage of the luxury of designing from scratch to adapt the floor plan, cabinets, appliances, or surfaces to your needs.

Look through Chapter One **for inspiration and ideas on the structural components, finishes, and surfaces** that create a design direction. In newer houses, kitchens are often parts of open plans so **you'll want to take the style** and color palette of adjoining rooms into consideration. Whether your project is a new kitchen, a remodeling, or just freshening up, Chapters Two through Five **showcase the latest ideas and trends in surfaces, storage, and dining and gathering**

areas. And when you like to do decorating projects yourself, turn to Chapter Six for **easy, effective solutions to common challenges.** Whether your kitchen is open to other rooms or is a contained space, **for design harmony decorate with materials, furnishings, and accessories that are compatible in spirit.** If your kitchen is a basic space with plain wood or painted cabinets, use it as a blank canvas to **create a definite style.** For example, if your style is American or French Country, **introduce colors, fabrics, furnishings, and collectibles that reinforce your interests.** By simply washing the walls with warm yellow paint, hanging French blue printed cafe curtains, and adding French-style caned chairs or barstools, your kitchen will reflect the warmth of the South of France.

findyourstyle

Decorating is personal—especially for informal spaces such as the kitchen. Before you start decorating, assess what you plan to keep, what you want to change, and determine the look that appeals to you. The decorating ideal is to reflect your own preferences rather than to strictly interpret defined styles. If you love country or Scandinavian, for example, incorporate those elements into your kitchen, and don't worry about an exact design-school or historical interpretation. As an ultimate goal, plan a decorating project that integrates your kitchen into your whole-house scheme. Together, well-chosen cabinets, surfaces, wall colors, and furnishings plus accessories create your style. Whether you enjoy traditional or contemporary, give yourself the option of relaxing or warming the mood for your kitchen. In a house with traditional furnishings, create a cozy space with a paint color chosen from window treatment fabric, or opt for wallpaper. Furnish the room with less formal classic pieces, such as Windsor or ladder-back chairs. To warm a house of modern classics and pared-down contemporary furnishings, introduce vibrant kitchen color with paint, cabinets, or playful furnishings, such as a stylized wall clock. As a transition from a neutral palette in your dining room to the kitchen, for example, repeat one or more of the neutrals but enliven the space with a jolt of dramatic color.

findyourstyle

Enliven sleek, mid-20th-century cabinetry with eye-catching, unexpected color and furnishings.

COLORS OF CONTEMPORARY. Unlock your imagination to experience the joy of lively color. Take advantage of the color wheel by choosing neighboring colors for wall-hung and base cabinets. For the best results when updating metal cabinets, consult with an automobile painting firm or a company that specializes in repainting kitchen appliances.

Metal kitchen cabinets with the original pulls, *right,* are icons of mass production of the 1930s through the '50s and are gaining new respect. Painted glossy apple green and blueberry, these once-drab cabinets set the spirited design tone for a stylish, suburban kitchen. Brick-shape black ceramic tiles, trimmed with '50s-style decorative tiles, clad the long expanse of backsplash. The natural tongue-and-groove wall paneling and pendent lighting recall popular '50s American ranch-style design, while shapely bar chairs and artful candlesticks introduce worldly European-inspired accents.

FANCY DRESS COTTAGE. Enjoy your love of cottage style in your kitchen as well as in your home's more formal rooms. If you crave the details, fabrics, and collections of this appealing style, decorate your kitchen to reflect your taste and furnishings. Incorporate an antique or well-styled reproduction secretary, cupboard, or Welsh dresser for storage and collectible display. Base the scale of the piece on the size of your kitchen. If your kitchen is spacious, include an upholstered chair or two for neighborly chats.

▲ Lighthearted, hand-painted floral details, *above left,* dress the paneled back door in the style of miniature framed paintings. The delicate, old-fashioned design repeats as accents for the radiator cover with detailed edges. The classic checkerboard floor of 16-inch-square porcelain tiles recalls Victorian-era kitchens. The fresh white shelves contrast with the taupe and yellow walls.

▲ The antique Georgian secretary relocates from the living room to the kitchen, *above right,* for a convenient writing surface and organizer. The top displays a cachepot. The slipper chair, in a lively windowpane check, introduces a touch of the Edwardian, the decorative and historical period that followed Victorian. A rack for mugs and blue willow plates decorate the walls above the chair rail.

▲ Wallpaper refreshes the walls above the chair rail, *opposite,* while the lower wall is painted a soft chamois shade. Padded cornices, covered in a classical-motif fabric, conceal the tops of operable Austrian shades. The motifs from the fabric repeat as photocopied cutouts pasted to the lower walls. A skirt hides storage under the corner shelf. The iron chandeliers illuminate in style.

SMALL-SPACE CHIC. Think of a small kitchen as the ideal opportunity to enrich surfaces without breaking your decorating budget. When space is limited, use stone or solid-surfacing materials for the backsplash as well as the countertop. Match upper and lower cabinets to avoid dividing the space. Choose white paint, distressed finishes, or light wood, such as natural maple, to keep a small kitchen as open as possible. Minimize countertop accessories and opt for clear canisters to avoid visual clutter. If possible, leave windows uncovered or dress with simple shades or blinds if privacy or sun control are concerns.

▲ To-the-ceiling plain cabinets above decorative glass doors, *opposite,* visually enlarge a small, L-shape kitchen in an older city house. The traditional, paneled details and classic brass knobs enhance the white cabinets. Granite countertops, neatly trimmed with a bullnose edge, extend to the backsplash as a seamless surface. Faux-stone laminate is another option.

▲ The painted black diamonds create a checkerboard pattern, *above,* that refreshes a worn pine floor. Diamonds were taped off and painted with black porch enamel. Polyurethane seals the floor for durability. A small writing table pairs with two reproduction chairs for dining and visiting.

▲ Built-ins sized to specific needs, such space for this portable television, *left,* are a must in a compact kitchen. The wine rack above keeps favorite vintages at hand.

ASIAN MEETS ITALIAN. Erase the borders of design and savor a kitchen that showcases current influences from a variety of sources. Creatively mix and match graphic design influences and materials—American Arts and Crafts, chic Italian, and natural and serene Asian.

In this multicultural kitchen, *above,* the natural maple cabinets with grid detailing allude to American Shaker and Craftsman influences. Botanical prints, stacked in pairs, reinforce the strong grid. The flooring is Italian tile. Japanese screens inspired the pot rack, while chrome Greek fisherman lights illuminate the scene.

The painted celadon walls pair with maple cabinetry and granite surfaces to create a quiet background for a busy cook's kitchen, *right.* Sea-sanded glass, mixed with clear glass, gives an opaque look for concealed storage and introduces another visual element. Muntin bars detailing the cabinet doors echo the grid on the island and its extra-deep drawers. Softly gathered drapery sheers soften the door to the garden. In contrast to the Shaker-influenced straight lines and precise angles of the room, the round breakfast table and a tropical woven wicker chair relax the tailored design with a more casual feel.

▲ The gently curved, granite-clad island bar, *above,* recalls the open kitchens of chic contemporary bistros. The open, cube storage area, topped with a butcher-block work surface, includes a handy wine rack. The woven bar chairs are in the style of a contemporary classic. Celadon bowls in the Asian style are symmetrically displayed above the commercial-style range.

▲ Replicating a cafe's food preparation area, *left,* wall sconces light the glass storage shelf and soapstone work counter. Curved handles detail sleek drawer fronts. Open bottom shelves are sized to fit tall woven rush baskets.

UPDATED VICTORIAN. If you live in an older home or enjoy charming Victorian style, plan a combination kitchen, dining, and sitting area that exemplifies your interests. Feel free to mix materials, finishes, patterns, and furniture. Work with a cabinetmaker to construct or enhance cabinets with period detailing. Look through architectural history books to understand the mix of countries and eras that influenced Victorian style. Or transform a standard kitchen by painting or stenciling cabinets with period motifs, such as Gothic arches. Deepen the flavor with period reproduction wallpaper and patterned fabrics in the rich colors of the period. Replace standard lighting with a vintage or reproduction chandelier.

▲ A melding of French and English influences as seen in the mix of cabinet styles, *opposite,* aptly illustrates the Victorian penchant for eclectic interiors—and the current popularity of unfitted kitchens. (Unfitted refers to furniture-quality cabinets that may or may not match.) The mix of stain colors, carved trims, and hand-painted details on the cabinetry personalizes a large dine-in kitchen. Enameled metal bar chairs lighten the look with more contemporary styling.

▲ The built-in breakfront with Gothic-style doors and applied carving, *left,* turns convenient storage into a decorative focal point. Reproduction spindle-back chairs and the nailhead tabletop reinforce the striking translation of period style to a 21st-century family kitchen. The floor's inlaid tiles, with a mosaic border, brighten the space as do the luminous yellow walls.

▲ Layers of pattern in the sitting area, *below,* from wallpaper to fabrics, emulate 19th-century morning rooms. The secretary and Oriental-style chair provide a handy spot for household accounts. The canine collection pays homage to the English love of dogs.

MOSAIC OF RAINBOW COLORS. Personalize your kitchen decorating with your favorite colors. When you decorate with colorful tiles, instead of relying solely on wall paint, you'll have the pleasure of choosing appealing crayon-bright colors. Visit a tile store or home center to survey the colors of standard ceramic tile. For the boldest look, tile the backsplash and heavy-use areas, such as behind the cooktop, as well as sections of the countertops.

▲ The granite top for the center island, *above,* provides an attractive, neutral surface in contrast to the colorful tile countertops. A gentle arch details the open shelves, designed for cookbooks and family memorabilia. Plain wood stools blend into the colorful space.

▲ Beaded-board cabinet doors with decorative knobs contribute old-fashioned charm to the decor, *opposite,* while polished metal drawer pulls add pleasing curved shapes. The arched glass doors dress up the space and echo the arch of the island's built-in.

▲ White grout frames the array of vibrant tiles, *above left,* without the distraction of a darker shade. The white helps to unify the open kitchen as it repeats the white of the cabinetry and woodwork. The tiles also work as a dramatic backdrop to accessories such as the sculptural bowl.

▲ Details, including the beaded trim on the drawer surrounds, *below left,* enhance the refined look of a kitchen planned for family living and entertaining. The decorative hardware and apron-front sink introduce European-inspired elements.

EUROPEAN COUNTRY. Partake of the pleasures of the Old World in a kitchen planned and decorated for dining and casually elegant entertaining. If space allows, incorporate an island or peninsula for guests to pitch in with cooking chores and a generous size table for lingering over after-dinner coffee. Include a mix of warm, mellow wood finishes in your designs. For an existing kitchen, accent the European look with elements such as a rustic dining table, plate rack, glass doors in a section of cabinets, olive jars, pottery pieces, and decorative bottles of oils and vinegars.

Maple cabinets, sealed with three wood stains, *above*, echo the relaxed look of a farmhouse kitchen that time has gently revised and enriched. The subtle arch of the built-in china cabinet tops the side units and the open decorative shelving. The cabinet serves as a hutch for tableware, linens, and serving pieces. To balance the ceiling height, the storage pantry cabinet's pointed top alludes to Gothic furniture styles. The kitchen's generous proportions allow room for

a detailed cabinet over the refrigerator. Open shelving below the cabinet balances a built-in that houses the microwave. More utilitarian base cabinets sport two finishes and a mix of knobs and pulls. The blend of old shelves, glass doors, and island storage contribute to the organized storage that is anything but standard issue.

▲ Sturdy metal chairs, detailed with cutouts of the Lone Star of Texas, *above,* invite family and friends to gather and visit with the cook. For the fun of mixing not matching, Country-French-style, painted reproduction dining chairs contrast with a rustic dining table constructed from recycled wood. Backsplash tiles laid on the diagonal and solid-surface countertops provide background for the rich mix of finishes and accessories. Glazed pottery pieces, chosen for their large scale in the generously sized room, strengthen the European country ambience. The vaulted ceiling allows space above the cabinets for display. An ornamental wall-hung birdcage presides over the diverse mix of accessories.

White beadboard trimming the peninsula and Windsor-style bar chairs, *left,* brighten the green and contrast with the painted tongue-and-groove ceiling. Butcher block clads the countertop. The woven rag rugs, over poplar flooring, add summer-fresh accents. Cup hooks, under the open double shelving, reinforce country style.

From the painted cabinets to the crockery jar, *opposite, top left,* green cools this lakeside kitchen with fresh-air ambience. Glass doors with muntin bars transform practical white dinnerware, pitchers, and tea- and coffeepots into decorative accessories.

The green metal roasting pan on the open shelf, *opposite, top right,* found at a flea market, inspired the green palette and country decorating scheme. The vintage white enamel oven, still in use, strengthens the early-20th-century mood of the family retreat. The open shelves and rack for pots keep everyday necessities and tools at hand. The bread box adds storage.

An old-fashioned plate rack, crafted from salvaged cast-iron gateposts, *opposite, bottom left,* encourages family and guests to help themselves—and makes putting up dishes a breeze. The plain white dishes and canisters add interesting shapes without the distraction of color or pattern.

Painted to match the cabinets and ceiling, a salvaged oar, *opposite, bottom right,* hangs between French doors as an ode to summer at the lake. The vintage, apron-style porcelain sink, from England, pairs with reproduction hardware. (Similar reproduction sinks are available.) Metal bin pulls and latch-type hardware on the base cabinets recall cottage farmhouses.

AT THE LAKE. Enjoy the ease of vacation living throughout the year with the colors, finishes, furnishings, and details of a lakeside retreat. Start with medium green for the painted surfaces and pair the color with light natural woods and crisp, spiffy white. Decorate with cabin collectibles. Plan storage so sturdy white plates, cups, and glasses contribute to the decorating.

COMMERCIAL MEETS COUNTRY. Define style your way when planning and decorating your kitchen. Choose the elements that fit your space and work with how you use your kitchen. When the kitchen is a busy hub for cooking and entertaining, incorporate commercial-quality finishes, shelving, and appliances with welcoming country touches such as recycled wood and vintage storage units.

▲ The exposed ceiling with hanging metal pendent lighting and wide heart-pine plank flooring, *opposite top,* emulates trendy bistro-style restaurants. Well-made stock manufactured base cabinets provide concealed storage; open shelving replaces wall-hung cabinets. Old and new mix stylishly—from the ladder, suspended from the ceiling as a pot rack—to the glass-front commercial refrigerator. A poured concrete counter tops the corrugated-steel-clad center island/breakfast bar.

▲ A commercial steel prep table rolls to where the action is, *right.* Flat baskets encourage recycling. The vintage plate rack contributes its own bistro touch as does the new metal shelving, including a floor-to-ceiling unit, built on site.

▲ Commercial handles receive a residential application as the pulls for the narrow, pullout spice shelves, *opposite, bottom left,* that flank the cooktop. The concrete countertop contrasts with the wood and steel textures. The sealed surface is safe for hot pans.

▲ The granite, apron-style sink pairs with an old-fashioned tub set, *opposite, bottom right,* to make washing large pots an easier chore. Corrugated shower glass, attached with silicone caulk, protects the wall to either side of the granite backsplash. An open shelf with a guard rim conveniently holds drinking glasses.

LOW COUNTRY AMBIENCE. Emulate the Low Country of the Carolina coast for kitchen decorating that exudes warmth and personality. For the best of this inviting style, combine natural wood finishes, vintage materials, a French decorative detail or two—and a comfortable gathering place to graciously welcome guests and family.

▲ Moderate in size, this L-shape kitchen, *above,* includes a center food preparation island that doubles as a breakfast bar. With the sink located in the center island, the cook enjoys being part of the convivial atmosphere. As a budget-stretcher, granite clads only the island; countertops are sealed recycled pine flooring. The French-style oven hood and plate rack are pine to match the cabinets.

▲ Salvaged decorative architectural trim, *top right,* imparts a one-of-a-kind focal point to the built-in cupboard. Painted details add subtle touches of color and texture to a muted, natural-wood scheme.

▲ A built-in storage unit, with pilaster (half column) detailing to replicate the base cabinets, conceals pantry storage and shelves for dinnerware, *center right.* Stylish and lightweight metal and woven-seat barstools easily slide under the island extension when not in use.

▲ In the best of Low Country style, the pine cabinets feature wood knobs and simple paneled detailing, *bottom right.* Miniature prints, matted and framed, turn the backsplash into an art display. A mosaic pitcher, crafted from pottery shards, neatly corrals wooden utensils.

CLASSIC BLUE AND WHITE. Decorate your kitchen in this beloved color combination for a look that's always fresh and inviting. Start with white cabinetry and choose surfaces and accessories that enhance. Edit your fabrics and finishing touches to shades of blue and white for a versatile scheme.

▲ Old-fashioned, hexagon-shape floor tiles, *below*, top the counter in this redecorated cottage kitchen. The pointed edge of the tile works as the counter edge, with the repetition of blue and white. The brass towel rack adds a dressy touch.

▲ Blue and white wallpaper, on the ceiling as well as the walls, *opposite*, gives a unified, open look, underscored by the beaded-board cabinet doors and white appliances. For maximum storage in the small space, cabinets extend to the ceiling. Durable, looped rugs on the old heart-pine floor echo the blue and white scheme and offer the contrast of an abstract pattern in the cottage setting. White light fixtures and an accent lamp provide balanced illumination. Art decoration is limited to collected plates, including the blue willow that sets the scheme.

▲ Finely detailed blue and white porcelain cabinet knobs, *above*, dress up the cabinetry with pretty details. Even the tea towels enhance the popular palette.

▲ Charming accessories, such as the imported cottage canisters, *left*, impart personality and give storage without clutter in a small kitchen. While surfaces, details, and accessories are blue and white or white, the canisters, coffee mugs, and accent lamp brighten with touches of yellow. The classic white pitcher, used for flowers as well as beverages, and white bowls are practical as well as stylish.

surfaces

If your goal is a simple freshening up, start by painting the walls or cabinets for an instant update. For projects that involve planning a new or remodeled kitchen, consider the impact of style-making countertops and flooring. Survey the choices of materials for counters and base your choice on style as well as budget. The four most common options you'll see are laminate, solid-surface material, tile, and granite. Stainless steel, butcher block, and concrete provide individualized looks and can be used for selected areas and for general countertops. Granite is a durable, handsome material; granite tile is a lower-cost alternative. As a budget-stretcher, combine two different countertop materials. Select the more expensive tile or granite for an island and finish with laminate for the countertops. Or check with resurfacing companies that apply top coats to change the color of standard laminate. Because flooring is a long-term change, look at wood and tile as well as vinyl or true linoleum floors. If you decide on vinyl, choose neutral colors and minimal pattern for a backdrop. Wall color can be anything but neutral. Paint is quick to apply and economical so throw out preconceptions and choose a favorite shade or lively decorative finish. Consider color for cabinets, too. Blue and green, as well as barn red, are traditional favorites. Look at opaque stains and glazes as well as durable oil-based paints.

surfaces

For a kitchen that welcomes guests with style, assemble a palette of artfully aged surfaces, happy colors, and practical, durable finishes.

DECORATE WITH TILE. Energize a plain ceramic tile backsplash and counter with decorative tile as trim and insets. If you have specific motifs in mind, consult with a local artist who works with tile. Or shop home centers and tile stores for a variety of shapes, styles, and colors.

A mix of tiles works well for durable, easy-to-clean kitchen surfaces, *right*. To warm the cool look of three tile surfaces plus the tile kitchen table, the saltillo clay floor tile introduces a charming handmade material. Decorative tiles, such as the fruit-motif border and insets, accent the white backsplash and counter. To unify the botanical theme, the tile-topped table pairs with vegetable-motif cushions. The antiqued, glazed finish for the cabinets blends softer, subtle tints. Glazed drawer pulls match, rather than contrast.

WOOD AND STONE. Here's a simple way to select surfaces: Choose darker stains for wood surfaces to make a kitchen feel cozier, and choose white or light finishes and surfaces to open up the space. Textured surfaces, such as clay tile and stone, warm a kitchen and lend an air of rustic appeal. An interesting paint color, rather than a neutral shade, animates as a strong design statement. A final caveat: It's prudent to base the number of contrasting finishes on the size of your kitchen. A mix of surface materials personalizes an open, spacious kitchen/family room but overpowers a small kitchen.

▲ Stacked fieldstone, *below*, incorporated into the cooking hearth as a durable, heat-resistant surface, recalls the inviting kitchens of Italy and France.

▲ Green walls and a coffered ceiling unify the kitchen and family living area, *above*. A decorative wood column in the bay window repeats the rich wood tones. Classic stained cabinets contrast with the more contemporary look of white, solid-surface material countertops. Tumbled marble tiles contribute texture and natural colorations.

▲ White and natural wood materials balance a kitchen of diverse surfaces, *opposite*. Mossy green walls, recalling the outdoors, bridge the contrast between the diverse colors and materials. The tile, laid on the diagonal, and the stacked stone introduce pattern in a kitchen where appeal comes from surface textures.

FURNITURE QUALITY. Look to unfitted English and European kitchens for design inspiration. In this handsome style, craftspeople design and build cabinets with the proportions, lines, and detailing of fine furniture. Quality and individuality, rather than matching storage cabinetry, are the goals. Cabinets can be constructed of different woods— or a combination of natural wood and painted finishes. Stone countertops mix with fine wood craftsmanship, as granite is often chosen for its durability and beauty. Decorative, rounded edges smooth the stone and transform it into sleek tabletops for dining as well as sturdy surfaces for cooking and baking.

Faux-stone detailing, created from wood and paint, flanks the built-in armoire storage in a kitchen planned for dining and entertaining, *opposite*. In the recessed butler's pantry, a painted paneled cabinet adds convenient concealed storage while open shelves, highlighted by arches, keep glassware at hand. Overhead arches provide decorative display.

On the painted wood backsplash above the granite trim, *above,* cups swing casually from bistro-style metal hooks. A damask tea towel hangs neatly from a copper rod. Practical classic terra-cotta pots and serving pieces and a rush basket accent with simplicity.

Details do make a difference in kitchen decorating, *opposite.* Bracket supports on the counter extension and raised-paneling trim on the frameless cabinets lend cottage charm to the contemporary open floor plan. The painted stools add a personal welcoming touch, as does a collection of American pottery—including salt-glazed crocks to stylishly organize utensils.

A window seat, *below,* doubles as convenient storage—with open shelves for baskets—as well as a cozy gathering spot for afternoon tea. A tightly woven cotton fabric in a casual print stands up to everyday wear in a busy family kitchen. Shirred detailing dresses the seat cushion while accent pillows enhance the charm of the relaxed, yet polished area.

WARMING STAINLESS STEEL.

To design a kitchen with a clean, unified look, pair commercial-quality stainless steel countertops with stainless steel appliances. Depending on your needs and space, shop for restaurant-style or residential ovens and refrigerators.

In this traditional, yet tailored kitchen, *above,* painted cabinets balance the industrial style of the coolly sleek steel countertops. The decorative glass doors, painted beaded-board for the backsplash, and a Roman fabric shade also warm the industrial material. Framed prints leaned against the backsplash visually soften the decorating mood. Frames are distressed gold for a casually sophisticated touch.

surfaces

SLEEK SURFACES. Think spare, not bare, when designing and decorating a contemporary kitchen. For personality and color, choose selectively from the ever-increasing variety of modern accessories. Arrange one or two large-scale pieces, such as pottery and wire baskets, to make a strong, uncluttered design statement.

▲ Natural wood cabinet doors with chrome pulls set the modernist mood in the spacious kitchen, *opposite.* Black—as the granite countertops and cabinet trim—reinforces the design allusions to sophisticated mid-20th-century design. Recessed lighting on dimmers and white walls complete the pared-down look.

▲ Restaurant-style metal corner shelving, *below,* introduces a quirky, but functional, accent into a cool contemporary space and allows colorful pottery dishes to brighten the work area. Well-polished copper canisters and the pottery displayed on the upper shelf warm the shiny metal surfaces for an inviting welcome.

TRIMMED TO SIMPLICITY. If you prefer your kitchen as a canvas for changing accessories and art, consider the possibilities of ever-fashionable and versatile white walls and cabinetry. For enriched design interest, work in detailing such as trim, raised paneling, decorative pulls and tiles, and touches of natural, unpainted wood. Include glass doors and open shelving to store and display colorful kitchenware, accessories, and seasonal decoration, and an all-white kitchen will be filled with color and infused with personal, ever-changing charm.

▲ Natural wood, such as the shelves for cookbooks, *opposite, left*, breaks up the visual monotony of an all-white space. In a typical open plan with an adjacent family room, raised paneling enhances design interest and recalls the Craftsman style of classic American bungalows.

▲ Fewer, larger accessories and art, *above center*, make a strong statement in kitchens as they do throughout the house. A framed art poster works well in the kitchen and is more striking than typical kitchen prints. The basket accents with texture while the Oriental rug provides balance and color. Windsor-style chairs, beautiful in their classic simplicity, complement the serene backdrop and are timeless investment pieces.

▲ White kitchens naturally welcome colorful accessories, *above right*. Inset vegetable tiles above the stove and whimsical teatime cabinet pulls personalize the kitchen. Open shelves, constructed from natural wood, are sized cube-style to neatly organize cookbooks and accessories. Cabinets flanking the stove include adjustable shelves for convenient storage and display of a variety of dinnerware, glasses, and oversize serving pieces.

COUNTRY FRENCH CHIC.
Think warm colors and earthy
texture to plan a kitchen in the
decorating spirit of Provence.
For the most appropriate
decorating look, combine textured
wall finishes, earthy clay tiles, and
wood stains in deep fruitwood
tones. Include motifs associated
with French design, such as
appealing farm animals.

Kitchens with definite style call
for striking design. In a reflection of
all things French, this kitchen boldly
melds textured paint finishes, colors,
wood tones and finishes, tiles, and
detailing, *opposite*. As an effective,
yet easy design idea, beaded board
painted a vivid accent color covers
the back of the open wall-hung
cabinet. Baskets add chic yet
accessible island storage.

The well-edited touches of dark
green, *above,* accent the neutral
kitchen and contrast with the
collection of rooster plates and the
ceramic rooster. Rooster tiles, set into
the plaster, personalize the work area.
Casement windows, in French style,
embellish with the warmth of wood.

A smattering of hand-painted
tiles in the rooster motif, *above right,*
contrast with the diagonally set
terra-cotta tiles.

PAPERS AND PATTERNS. Wallpaper, fabric, and even flooring laid in a pattern animate stylish kitchen decorating.

▲ The scored concrete floor, *above,* emulates tile in a European-style kitchen. Decorative molding trims cabinets.

▲ A hand-painted mural, *top right,* repeats the country blue of the painted beaded-board cabinet below. The plaid valance contrasts with the stripes of the chandelier shades.

▲ A lively floral wallpaper energizes a classic black and white kitchen—and proves the big impact of just a touch of the right pattern, *right.* The pennant-style valances and the chair seats, sewn from a lively check, freshen the crisp design.

▲ Dressy wallpaper, such as this floral typically used in dining rooms, enriches with art-quality details, *opposite, top left.* Art hung on a cabinet contributes color and motif.

▲ Ceramic tiles in a checkerboard pattern, *opposite, top right,* update a compact kitchen. Stained glass above the sink revives with color—especially when the sun shines.

▲ Cork, popular in the '30s, returns to the design scene as it creates artful inlaid flooring patterns, *opposite, bottom left.*

▲ Classic wallpaper, such as the ticking pattern on the walls and ceiling, *opposite, bottom right,* transforms the kitchen's dining area into a cozy, country cottage retreat.

storage&display

Open and closed are the two key words in kitchen storage. Start with cabinets as the major investment for **function and style.** If new cabinets are in your plan, consider a combination of dark and light wood finishes—or of **painted and stained surfaces.** Varying the colors or tones and the detailing offers visual relief in a kitchen with lots of built-in storage. Or **mix glass-door cabinets and open shelving** with cabinets that feature solid doors. When updating or refreshing an existing kitchen, paint or re-stain older cabinets. Prepare cabinets by removing doors and hardware before sanding. Use tack cloths to remove dust. If you paint previously stained cabinets, apply a deglazer to remove the glossy finish before priming. Although **oil-based paint** requires careful application and cleanup, it gives a durable, scrubbable surface. Add stylish new hardware as a finishing touch. As a **budget-stretcher,** select specialty hardware for the most visible wall-hung cabinets and choose compatible, basic pulls or knobs for base units. For additional storage, hang **open shelves or a plate rack** on the kitchen wall. For an extra work/storage area, purchase a cart on casters with open shelving. In a tiny kitchen, **think creatively of every space**—even inside the window frame—to attach open shelving. Or add a pot rack, hooks, pegs, or wall-mounted baskets for storage.

storage&display

**Mix cabinet finishes and shelving to create a cozy mood in an open kitchen.
Visually enlarge a small one with glass cabinet doors for display.**

**ACCENT WITH COLOR AND
LIGHTING.** Give your kitchen a stylish,
well-designed update by painting the
insides of glass-door cabinets the same
color as the walls. Add do-it-yourself
interior lighting strips for extra sparkle.

▲ This well-edited, compact kitchen
combines necessary storage with attractive
display, *right*. The secret? Eye-level glass-
door cabinets anchor the design while
solid-door cabinets that store infrequently
used items fit to the ceiling and below the
counter. The rich red stands out against
the white woodwork and repeats for the
red-banded window treatment. The marble
counter wraps around the wall for extra
display, and the cutting board slides under
the counter. White canisters for storing
everyday staples blend with the
backsplash and marble.

ENGLISH COTTAGE STYLE. Take inspiration from the beautifully constructed, furniture-quality cabinetry known as unfitted. To emulate this look, neatly combine open shelves, glass doors, solid doors, and a variety of basket and rack storage. Details, such as turned legs on the island and divided-light doors, enhance the English charm.

▲ Storage with style translates into an open display over both the sink and the cabinets, *above*. Details, such as drawers with classic white porcelain knobs under the island counter, strengthen the appealing design.

▲ Repetition of shapes and elements visually unifies a well-designed kitchen. The curves of the rusty-finish iron pot rack, hung for convenient and handsome storage, appear again on the dining lighting fixture, *left*. A variety of textures, such as the storage baskets, butcher-block island top and rusty iron, copper, and pottery accessories, warms the cool white and tile scheme.

FLOOR-TO-CEILING SOLUTIONS. When you enjoy collecting but space is tight, consider every inch of your wall fair game for storage and display. An antique cupboard, Welsh dresser, or china cabinet work well for fragile items, although such pieces aren't likely to have enough display area for extensive collections. As a space- and budget-stretching option, install shallow, open shelving on an interior wall. For stability, make sure the shelving is attached to the wall studs. If you plan to display plates or platters, have plate-rack-style grooves cut into some of the shelves for security.

▲ Designed to meld the materials, colors, and furnishings of the Southwest and the Northeast, this kitchen, *opposite left,* illustrates the warmth of personal design in the gathering space. As the kitchen has little concealed storage, built-in shelves, recessed between wall studs, corral cookbooks and pantry staples. A wall of floor-to-ceiling open shelving organizes a diverse display of serving pieces and collectibles. The display of American and European pieces recalls travels and family occasions. The top shelf, wider for stability, works well for heavier infrequently used pieces.

▲ For a one-of-a-kind look, cabinet doors, *above center,* detailed with tile, pair with drawers enlivened with an antiqued finish. Color provides the theme with green repeating—tile, painted and antiqued wood, lighting, and pottery. Clever design shows in the recessed open shelves for spices and the easy-to-maneuver, sturdy drawer pulls.

▲ A built-in work surface with storage drawers takes advantage of space below the window, *above right.* Wall-hung, to-the-ceiling cabinets maximize storage in a remodeled kitchen; the sink skirt neatly conceals utilitarian items.

COLORFUL AND CLEVER. Think outside narrow boundaries of standard kitchens as you design your personal space. When you work with a style theme, such as the Southwestern-influenced mood in this kitchen, choose storage and display that enhance your chosen look. Shop for practical items, such as metal shelving, hooks, and utensils, that are as handsome as they are functional.

▲ This design-savvy kitchen, *opposite*, maximizes every possible inch for handy storage. The microwave fits snugly in the island while a metal mesh shelf with hooks displays serving pieces and keeps utensils at hand.

▲ For striking display storage, painted cabinets flank open shelves with a built-in plate rack, *above*. The rusty red repeats visually as the recessed shelves and for the plate rack with painted dowels. The dramatic deep purple of the base cabinets works equaly well as the trim color for the window and the plate rack. Such repetition of vivid color unifies a diverse scheme. Wall space, even the backsplash area over the counter and the soffits, enlivens the scene.

MIXING STYLES AND MATERIALS.

The trend to larger, more open kitchens and dining areas is accompanied by storage challenges: How do you avoid the institutional look of walls of cabinets? As a practical solution, designers advocate introducing a variety of finishes and pulls for cabinets and drawers. This allows you to enjoy the crisp appeal of white cabinets, the warmth of natural wood finishes, and the easy care of laminate surfaces. Glass doors, used judiciously, complete the mix.

▲ Leaded glass doors dress up lighted cabinets used to store glassware, *below left*. Painted tongue-and-groove doors with glass knobs enrich handcrafted base cabinets and drawers.

▲ Glass doors with divided lights update a traditional-style kitchen, *right*. Open shelves, supported by iron brackets, provide accessible storage for items used every day and introduce an informal note in a large kitchen and dining area.

▲ Natural wood trim warms durable laminate drawer fronts, *below right*. Sturdy brass pulls finish in classic style.

▲ A mix of open and concealed storage—and glass and solid doors— works well in this kitchen planned for entertaining, *opposite*. A shallow cabinet under the island displays collectibles.

CONTEMPORARY ALTERNATIVES.

When modern is your style, the kitchen provides the ideal venue. Sleek looks in stock cabinetry are widely available for building or remodeling. Or if you update, consider such features as sliding wavy-glass cabinet doors for a modernist take on kitchen design.

▲ Pared-down materials and a neutral color palette team for the serene background associated with the best of contemporary design, *opposite.* Tambour-style doors for appliance garages reduce visual clutter, key to a clean, contemporary look. White walls, paired with natural wood tones, work as a neutral canvas for neatly arranged art. Glassware and dishes are strictly limited to clear, tinted, and white.

▲ Dark laminate countertops, trimmed in stained wood, anchor the airy kitchen, *above,* and contrast with the light natural wood. The wood trim, tambour doors, and open shelves create a striking design focus. The wavy, translucent glass diffuses and refracts light for interest, and requires a neat, organized, uncluttered approach for attractive storage. Open shelves are sized for a collection of fine art pottery, collected from art fairs. Such carefully selected collections warm and personalize contemporary design.

CLEANED UP FOR COMPANY. If you like to entertain family and friends in your kitchen, include a mix of concealed storage for the necessities: glass doors to show off your china, glassware, and serving pieces, and special touches, such as a built-in wine rack.

▲ In a kitchen where guests gather, *below left*, the owners concentrated concealed, utilitarian storage in the meal preparation area. Cabinets above the refrigerator and stove contain rarely used items. Open shelving, lighted from above, decoratively fills a corner.

▲ Divided-light glass doors, *above right,* solve the visual problem of a large wall of cabinets. For extra serving pieces, a third cabinet built over the cased opening provides accessible storage. Old-fashioned cup hooks, screwed inside some of the cabinets, add interest and the appeal of nicely shaped tea and coffee cups. Shiny brass knobs give a neat, handsome finish to the crisp painted wood.

▲ The generously sized built-in wine rack, *opposite,* lends a gracious note and introduces an interesting visual element to a kitchen planned with maximum open and closed storage. Although a pot rack isn't a space-saving necessity, the natural dowels and copper pots contrast with the white and granite surfaces. Little touches, such as the twig basket for vinegars and oils, warm and personalize while ensuring neat counters.

COLLECTORS' PARADISE. Decorate with your passions. You'll have inspiration for your color scheme, and your kitchen will tell your own personal story.

▲ Open shelving with beaded-board backings and decorative trim, *opposite, top left,* enhances a cottage-style kitchen; the skirt encourages neatly concealed storage.

▲ Green is the theme, *opposite, top right.* Vintage green glass mixes with green-handled kitchen utensils, pulls, and knobs on the dresser shelves and the wall above.

▲ Vibrant art glass, protected by acrylic cubes, enlivens a sleek, contemporary kitchen, *opposite, bottom left.*

▲ A custom-made plate rack, sized for dinner plates and saucers, *opposite, bottom right,* repeats the barley-twist detail that trims base cabinets. The pattern mix adds to the charm.

▲ An antique butcher block with drawers and wall-mounted pot hooks, *above left,* reinforces the colonial ambience.

▲ Glass doors, without muntins, and open corner shelving, *above right,* show off colorful everyday pottery. The vividly painted cabinets and shelves contrast as a colorful foil.

▲ The gently worn finish of the antique dresser, *left,* makes an appropriate rustic backdrop for a lighthearted mid-20th-century cowboy dinnerware collection. Cup hooks add display.

dining

Whether your kitchen is large or small, old or new, it's likely the gathering spot for family and friends. Everyone gravitates to the kitchen, **so make it the most inviting room of your home.** If you build or remodel, **include space for dining and sitting.** Built-in banquettes or cafe-style booths take advantage of corners and windows and can be designed to include extra storage and display, too. When space is tight, a cushioned window seat or padded banquette paired with a table **maximizes comfortable seating without crowding.** In larger open kitchens, bar-style seating at the island or peninsula as well as separate table and chairs are **gracious options.** Or, substitute a combination work and dining table for a center island. **American or European farm tables with chairs** are likely candidates, since they are sturdy and often include storage drawers. If you like the fashionable retro look, **shop secondhand and thrift stores** for a vintage 1950s-style chrome dining table and chairs—or shop mass market retail stores that sell mid-20th-century reproduction home furnishings. **In a small kitchen,** add a tiny bistro-style table and a pair of folding chairs that can be stored away when not needed. If your dining needs vary, look for a drop-leaf table or a small round table that can be expanded with a leaf. Or, purchase a compact, movable cart on casters that can work with **lightweight stools for instant seating.**

dining&gathering

Savor the space of an open kitchen plan with the versatility of a dining table that doubles as a work surface and for relaxed dining.

COUNTRY FRENCH CASUAL. Choose a table or design a kitchen island that reinforces the style and ambience of your dine-in kitchen. Unpolished woods welcome guests to country-style kitchens—and warm the sleek finishes of contemporary spaces, too. When you shop, look for sturdy reproduction or antique tables with simple lines and storage for everyday linens. If your cabinets are natural wood, consider the contrast of a painted kitchen table.

▲ In a kitchen with the luxury of space, two pine tables pair with painted cabinets, *right*. The simple tables relax the more high-style cabinetry that features raised-panel doors and handsome hardware. Seating mixes antique ladder-back chairs, including an armchair for the writing table, with an antique bench.

BANQUETTE BEAUTIFUL. Include built-in banquette seating for a dual dining and sitting spot that is a perfect homework corner, too. A sunny exposure welcomes guests and turns a corner into a gathering area. Include built-in display and storage—such as wide windowsills for plants—to take advantage of this addition.

▲ The softly curved banquette reinterprets the gentle lines of this European-inspired kitchen, *left,* and updates a traditional pedestal table and French-style chairs. The window cornice and wall-hung cabinets complement the design, as does the wall-mounted corner shelf. A floral print repeats for the padded banquette cushion and the shade above.

▲ The handsome cabinets, finished with a soft antique glaze, *above,* initiated the design and the palette for the dining area. Subtle finishes work well in large kitchens as they visually downplay expanses of storage. The pendent-style fixture repeats the traditional styling of the chandelier in the adjacent dining area.

▲ The clay-tile floor, laid in a modified herringbone pattern, *left,* extends from the kitchen into the dining area. Busy family dining and gathering spaces necessitate such durable and attractive flooring. Tile also recalls the French and Italian origins of popular design and blends well with American and European country looks.

JAZZ-CLUB CONTEMPORARY. Look at loft design for a thoroughly open floor plan that's ideal for pared-down modern decor. If your kitchen, dining, and living room are one space, plan for multiple gathering spots—such as barstools or chairs at a counter, a nearby separate dining area, and comfortable, upholstered seating.

The grid design of these contemporary chairs, *below,* repeats the pale, natural finish of the unadorned cabinets. Chairs and barstools in the same design visually unify and calm open, shared spaces.

Intense color integrates the kitchen, dining, and sitting areas of this open kitchen, *opposite.* The cobalt blue accent wall sets the design scheme with a jolt of high-powered color drama. The blue and terra-cotta seat cushions energize with a graphic, stylized pattern. Typical of a loft-style plan, the dining area pulls double duty as a gallery display of large-scale art, illuminated by sleek recessed lighting and the pendent fixture. The table, a stylized base with a tinted glass top, echoes the blue tone as an art piece in its own right. Accessories are minimized in the sleek look.

CLEAN COTTAGE STYLE. Work in a window seat for comfortable—and space-stretching—seating for your kitchen. Enjoy the enticing spot for morning coffee and the newspaper, and take advantage of the extra seating by pairing it with a dining table and chairs. If space is tight, consider a folding patio table and chairs that can be stored between meals.

▲ Creamy white enamel updates and unifies a turn-of-the-century oak table and mid-20th-century faux-bamboo chairs, *above*. Cafe curtains pair with a gathered valance for a window treatment that's ideal for daytime natural light and nighttime privacy. For the energy of contrast, the window seat fabric sports a plaid in the same cheerful colors as the floral.

▲ A comfortable armchair, cushioned, *above,* or upholstered, invites visitors and family to linger in a pretty kitchen. The fruitwood finish of the chair frame warms the white kitchen with a touch of natural wood. The repetition of the airy floral for the armchair, the kitchen's Roman shade above the sink, and cafe curtains and valance in the dining area stylishly meld the decorating scheme. The wall color repeats a shade of green from the floral fabric—another step to unified design. The easy-care rag rug softens the natural wood floor in the work area. Such a light, country-fresh scheme of creamy whites and pretty botanical-influenced colors provides a seamless solution to blending new and old furnishings in an updated space.

IN THE GARDEN STYLE.

Decorate your kitchen in the popular, airy garden style, and you'll have an easy solution for dining. When space is limited, shop for a small patio or bistro table to mix with a pair of chairs.

▲ The kitchen proper, *left,* continues the garden-fresh theme of the dining area. The extra dining chair, added to the table when needed, finds a home under the window garden.

▲ A standard ladder-back chair, *below left,* takes on the freshness of spring with white paint and delicate, hand-painted details. Classic blue and white elements create fresh, easy-to-love decorating. Touches of yellow in the plaid cotton cushion fabric add a cheerful note appropriate to the style.

▲ The center island with sink, *right,* defines without blocking the work, storage, and dining areas in a compact yet open kitchen. The classic two-color scheme, with touches of pale yellow, supplies the light garden feel to the moderate space. The gathered sheers, topped by the decorative valance, diffuse morning light and provide privacy.

FAMILY FARMHOUSE. When your ideal kitchen recalls the keeping rooms of earlier times, work in the relaxed farmhouse style. Plan for inviting seating at the island and for a separate dining area for homework and visiting around the kitchen table. Choose comfortable cushioned chairs to invite relaxing. Add cushions to your bar chairs, too, for extra comfort and country accents.

▲ An open-background floral wallpaper and matching fabric create country style in the dine-in kitchen, *opposite.* The light, whitewash finish on the Windsor-style bar chairs blends with the cabinets and alludes to traditional milk paint. Reproduction chairs in 19th-century style pair with a simple farm table.

▲ Guests who gather at the island serve themselves at the corner bar that doubles as a butler's pantry, *above left.* A portable television in the storage cabinet means easy access to the morning and evening news.

▲ A built-in window seat, *above right,* transforms a kitchen corner into a welcoming spot for reading the newspaper and relaxing before dinner. For a lively mix, a tailored check fabric covers the seat cushions; piping adds detailing. Pillows in an array of sizes and prints animate the cheerful setting. When more than two dine at the table, the window seat converts to extra seating. As a summertime alternative, the cushion can be slipcovered in creamy white. In such a sunny spot, applied window film that blocks damaging rays is a wise investment because it decreases fabric fading.

GRACIOUS DINING TABLE. Enjoy the friendly atmosphere of the kitchen even more by combining it with the dining room. An open arrangement works beautifully for casual family living and for entertaining. When your kitchen table is your dining table, choose a size and style large and dressy enough for all your needs. If you are lucky enough to inherit or find an antique table, pair it with comfortable and sturdy reproduction chairs. New dining chairs are sized larger than more delicate antique chairs and hold up better to the rigors of everyday family life.

A simple farmhouse-style table with straight legs generously seats six, *above.* The modified wheat-sheaf chair backs work with such a country piece—or would mix with a more formal look. The garden-style chandelier brightens with a whimsical note.

An island with storage and display, *opposite,* serves as a visual demarcation between the kitchen proper and the dining area. The furniture-quality piece, with a butcher-block top for meal preparation and other chores, contributes an extra serving area for buffets and informal meals. A trio of drawers keeps silverware and linens handy for the table.

DINING EXTRAS. Think creatively to find space for dining in the kitchen. Size your table and chairs accordingly or include built-in seating to maximize seating options.

▲ An L-shape banquette, *opposite, top left,* transforms a nook into a diner-style spot for meals and conversation. Pendent lighting reinforces the sleek, mid-20th-century mood.

▲ The lunch counter returns, *opposite, top right,* as the solution to dining in a space-starved kitchen. Bentwood-style bar chairs with cushions guarantee comfort.

▲ The peninsula, *opposite, bottom left,* extends as a combination dining and work space in contemporary style.

▲ The center work island, *opposite, bottom right,* expands dining options beyond the farmhouse table and chairs.

▲ Even tight galley spaces, *right,* can include dining with such lightweight options as a tiny bistro table and chairs, which move easily to the deck or porch in mild weather.

▲ A curved banquette, *below left,* incorporates space-saving storage and display, and doubles as a room divider.

▲ Even a window provides a space-conscious seating option, *below right.* For dining options, a small table and a folding chair or two can be added as needed.

decoratingideas

kitchenprojects

Decorate your kitchen with colors, fabrics, and collections that reflect your own style preferences. Kitchen decorating is most successful when you have a decorating goal and a starting point in mind. If your kitchen needs several projects—fresh paint, new cabinets, new window treatments, for example—make a list and work in an orderly, logical fashion. Other projects, such as adding and whitewashing beaded board or painting the floors featured in this chapter, take more time and skills.

 Some projects, such as painting the walls or kitchen chairs in lively colors, are easy but can be time consuming. If your kitchen is in good condition but not exciting, choose a motif, such as checkerboard, and design complementary decorating projects. Be judicious with accessories and treat your kitchen to the editing you would give your living room. Focus collections and displays on themes and colors, such as yellow pottery or blue and white plates to hang on the wall. If you have space over the cabinets, create arrangements that enhance rather than overwhelm.

CHECKERBOARD BORDER

SKILL LEVEL
Intermediate

TIME
2 days

SUPPLIES
- Pale beige paint
- Large paintbrush
- Natural sea sponge
- Warm tan paint
- Level with printed ruler
- Colored pencil
- Pale gray paint
- Narrow masking tape
- Small paintbrush
- Charcoal gray paint
- Ivy-motif stencil
- Stencil brush
- Pale green stencil paint
- Crackle medium
- Glaze

CHECKERBOARD BORDER

A decorative paint finish and painted border enliven the white walls of a standard kitchen. (As an alternative, purchase a wallpaper border in your favorite motif.)

- **Choose the colors for your border and the background**. In this project, walls are painted pale beige, then sponged with a warm tan. Paint is standard latex.

- **For the border, determine the width**. Measure it with a level with printed ruler, and pencil in guidelines. Paint the overall band a pale gray (or your color choice). Choose the dimensions for your checkerboard pattern and draw the lines, using the level with printed ruler and the colored pencil. Tape off with narrow masking tape.

- **With a small brush**, paint every other check with charcoal gray (or your color choice).

- **Allow the checkered border to dry**. Tape ivy stencils in various configurations over the checks, and brush on pale green stencil paint.

- **If you prefer an aged look for the border**, apply a layer of crackle medium, following the manufacturer's directions. Allow to dry and finish with glaze.

STAR PLATE STENCIL

SKILL LEVEL

Intermediate

TIME

Afternoon

SUPPLIES

- Stencil of plate motif
- Tracing paper
- Stencil plastic
- Fine-tipped marker
- Opaque stencil board or poster board
- Graphite paper or carbon paper
- Crafts knife
- Extra blades
- Cutting board or self-healing cutting mat
- Pencils
- Blue painter's tape
- Stencil paints in your color choices
- Stencil brushes

STAR PLATE STENCIL

- **Choose a commercial stencil** with a plate motif.
- **If you prefer to make your own, trace a pattern** from a novelty print fabric or wallpaper, or draw your own. Simplify your design to make it into a stencil. Avoid detailing that is too large or oddly shaped as it will be difficult to copy.
- **Draw or outline your design on tracing paper.** Follow one of the two methods described below to transfer the design to tracing paper.
- **For translucent stencil plastic**, place the design underneath the stencil plastic and trace with a fine-tipped marker.
- **For opaque stencil board or poster board**, place your design on top of a sheet of graphite paper or carbon paper that is on top of the stencil board. Tape down all layers and trace.
- **Cut out the stencil design with a crafts knife.** Have extra blades on hand and switch to sharp blades as often as necessary. Always cut on a cutting board; self-healing cutting mats are available at arts and crafts stores.
- **To stencil a plate on a wall**, familiarize yourself with the stencil and overlays, if your commercial stencil includes them. Plan your colors and practice on poster board.
- **Center the first plate you plan to stencil,** and mark the location with faint pencil marks. If you stencil more than one plate, determine the exact placement before you start stenciling.

COLOR SCHEME
SKILL LEVEL
Beginner
TIME
Depends on
availability and
shopping resources

COLOR SCHEME

(ALSO PICTURED ON PAGES 22–23)

Tile enlivens your kitchen with permanent color and style. To get started, visit tile specialty stores and home centers. You'll see a wide range of styles, sizes, colors, finishes, and motifs.

■ **To create your own version of this colorful kitchen,** decide on a general color scheme. White plus a color is foolproof. However, for fun, consider the bold look shown here. Borrow samples, if possible, or buy a few tiles to experiment with arrangements in your kitchen.

■ **Or cut out paper tiles in colors you like and tape them to your backsplash, counter, or island.** Arrange and rearrange until you find colors and patterns that work for your decorating.

Tip: Custom-colored tiles, as shown here, are versatile because you can add fabrics with novelty patterns and other accessories for quick changes. If you like a mural effect, purchase prefired murals that can be professionally installed in your kitchen. Or pair white with one or two colors.

CHAIR BRIGHTS

SKILL LEVEL

Beginner

TIME

3 to 5 days
(due to drying time)

SUPPLIES

- Thrift store or
unfinished chairs
- Fine-grade
sandpaper
- Clean rags
- Tack cloths
- Paintbrushes
- Oil-based enamel or
latex paint
- Water-based
polyurethane (optional)

CHAIR BRIGHTS

Stamp your color personality on your kitchen by painting chairs in a mix of your favorite colors.

■ **Shop thrift stores for mixing and matching chairs with interesting details**. Or look for unfinished chairs in pleasing shapes. Vintage chairs should be sturdy and in paintable condition. Stained or painted chairs normally work fine if you sand rough spots. (It isn't necessary to strip painted or stained wood before painting.) Wood furniture with a plastic-type top coat is not paintable.

■ **Don't worry about chairs matching exactly**. Instead, look for compatible shapes and sizes. Feel free to mix two armchairs with two side chairs, for example.

■ **To prepare chairs for painting**, wipe off dust and grime with a damp rag. Allow to dry. Sand rough spots and wipe off with a tack cloth.

■ **Prime and allow to dry. Brush on paint**. Oil-based enamel gives a tough, scrubbable finish; however, latex paint is available in much wider choices of colors.

■ **Allow paint to dry**. Apply a second coat.

■ **If you use latex paint, allow it to dry thoroughly**. Seal by brushing on a sealant coat of water-based polyurethane.

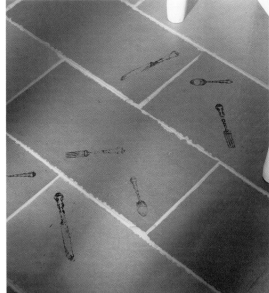

BROWN-BAG FLOOR

SKILL LEVEL

Intermediate

TIME

1 week (due to drying time)

SUPPLIES

- Assorted brown paper bags
- Ruler and scissors
- Enamel floor paint in your color choice (optional)
- Cardboard
- Vinyl-to-vinyl wallpaper paste
- Wallpaper roller
- Rubber stamps
- Enamel porch paint for stamping
- Water-based polyurethane
- Roller
- Paint tray

BROWN-BAG FLOOR

- **Collect brown paper bags from a variety of sources** for color variations.
- **Cut "tiles" to shape and size you prefer.** For the kitchen shown here, each tile is 7x13½ inches. The beige of the existing vinyl floor underneath mimics grout; wood or vinyl floors could be painted with enamel before paper is applied to emulate the look of grout. (Or overlay brown paper strips in random patterns.)
- **Cut a cardboard template** the size of the tile you prefer as a pattern to rip paper bags into rectangles. (This gives the pleasing handmade look of ragged, irregular edges.)
- **Spread vinyl-to-vinyl wallpaper paste** on the backs of the tiles, working with a few tiles at a time, and position them on the floor. Work out air pockets, and seal edges with a wallpaper roller. Allow the paste to dry thoroughly; time will vary.
- **Stamp the motif of your choice**, such as the tableware, *top right*. Seal with five coats of water-based polyurethane using a roller and paint tray.

FAUX-LINOLEUM FLOOR

SKILL LEVEL

Advanced

TIME

1 week
(due to drying time)

SUPPLIES

- Paper
- Colored papers
- White stain or white paint
- Straightedge
- Pencil
- Enamel floor paints
- Assorted small brushes
- Water-based polyurethane
- Roller
- Paint tray

FAUX-LINOLEUM FLOOR

- **Sketch on paper the design you have in mind.** Simple, stylized designs work best and are easier to emulate. For a unified design, **draw inspiration for the colors and patterns** you want to use from within your kitchen area.

- **Cut out squares of colored paper to size,** and lay them on the floor to determine the pattern and scale. Take your time. Vary blocks and patterns until you find what's pleasing to you.

- **Apply white stain to an unfinished floor or white paint over an already painted floor.** (If your floor has been sealed with polyurethane, check with a flooring company. You may need to sand and start with raw wood before staining.)

- **Lay out the floor pattern with a straightedge** and draw your guidelines with a pencil. The simpler the pattern, the easier the job.

- **Hand-paint the colored blocks or motifs with enamel paints.** Finish with one color before adding others. It's easier to paint large-scale blocks or patterns first and allow them to dry before detailing.

- **Seal with three or four coats of water-based polyurethane using a roller and paint tray.**

Tip: **Buy top-quality paintbrushes;** cheap brushes can shed bristles, potentially ruining a project.

COTTAGE STYLE

SKILL LEVEL

Intermediate

TIME

2 to 4 days

PANELING SUPPLIES

- Unfinished beaded-board paneling
- Nails
- Nail set
- Hammer
- Decorative molding cut for length of chair rail
- 1x2 cut for length of chair rail
- Enamel paint
- Small roller
- Paintbrush
- Paint tray

WALLPAPER SUPPLIES

- Patterned wallpaper
- Plumb bob or level
- Water box or wallpaper adhesive
- Wallpaper brush
- Sponges
- Utility knife
- Straightedge
- Seam roller

COTTAGE STYLE

Surface treatments and easy decorative accents can transform a contemporary kitchen into a cottage-style gathering spot.

- **Create wainscoting** by installing beaded-board paneling (shown 48-inches high) from a home center over drywall. Add a chair rail, constructed from decorative moldings and finished with a 1x2 cut to length. Finish with a pretty vintage-patterned wallpaper. (Open florals with an off-white, cream, linen, or pastel background are ideal for this look.)

- **Hang wallpaper in confined areas,** such as above a chair rail, if you are a novice. Before starting a project, plan how patterns will match. You will have to trim the last strip you put up to match the first strip. To minimize matching patterns, begin in an area that isn't obvious, such as a door or window.

- **Hang the first strip with absolute care.** Use a plumb bob (a small tool with a pullout string coated with chalk) or a level. Measure the width of the wallcovering from your starting point. Subtract ½-inch and mark your plumb line. Be sure to cut the strips so the pattern repeats match; the strips should be several inches longer than the finished height so the pattern repeats the match. Hang the first strip to the left of this line. Trim the strip for a perfect fit. To make sure the pattern repeats the match, cut the strips as you go—not all at one time.

- **If you use prepasted strips,** reroll with the patterned side in, starting from the bottom. Place the roll in a water box so the top of the strip comes out of the box. Place the box on the floor near the wall where the strip will be hung. Draw the roll up onto the wall and smooth it into position along the plumb line.

- **Smooth with a wallpaper brush or clean sponge** to eliminate air pockets. Double-check the position; trim excess with a sharp utility knife and a straightedge.

- **Carefully line the second strip up to the first.** Wait 15 minutes and smooth butted edges with a seam roller. Remove excess squeezed-out paste with a sponge and clean water.

- **To apply unpasted wallpaper, use the adhesive recommended by the manufacturer.** If you have questions, ask at the wallpaper store or home center. Place the first strip on a table, face down; spread adhesive on it from the center to the top edge. Fold the top half of the strip to the center, pasted surfaces together. Be careful not to crease. Repeat with the bottom half, following the same technique.

- **Hang the first strip** by opening the top half and lining up the pattern at the top. With a wallpaper brush, smooth to the wall; unfold and smooth the bottom half.

- **Deal with openings as you come to them.** Let the strip that adjoins the opening overlap door and window casings. Crease at the vertical edges and cut with a razor blade or extra-sharp knife. Be extremely careful; it's easy to slice a finger. Carefully crease and cut at the top of the casing, then for the casing beneath.

VINTAGE STYLE
SKILL LEVEL
Intermediate
TIME
2 days
SUPPLIES
- Unfinished beaded-board paneling
- Nails
- Nail set
- Hammer
- Fine-grade sandpaper
- Tack cloths
- Oil-based fruitwood stain with sealant
- Paintbrush
- White stain with sealant
- Clean cotton rags
- Window frame with glass panes
- Soft brush
- Commercial glass cleaner
- D-ring picture hooks
- Self-adhesive, clear, plastic album corners
- Cards, postcards, and other memorabilia

VINTAGE STYLE
As an alternative to painting beaded-board wainscoting, install and gently age unfinished wood with this quick antiqued finish. Pair with personal window wall art for the newest take on old-fashioned style.

- **Sand rough spots on installed paneling**, brush off dust, and wipe with a tack cloth.
- **Lightly brush on a coat of oil-based fruitwood stain with sealant**. Wipe off excess with a clean cotton rag. Allow to dry.
- **Brush on a coat of white stain with sealant**. For a pickled look, rub off excess with a clean cotton rag until you achieve the desired effect.
- **Purchase a window frame with intact glass panes, as shown.** Brush off dirt and loose paint. If necessary, clean with a soft brush dipped in a mild, sudsy solution. Wipe off with clear water and allow to dry. Clean glass with commercial glass cleaner.
- **To hang, attach D-ring picture hooks**, one on each side, to the top back of the window frame.
- **Press self-adhesive, clear-plastic picture-album corners** on the glass panes to display cards, postcards, or other memorabilia.

ROMANTIC-STYLE SURFACES SKILL LEVEL

Advanced

TIME

5 to 6 days
(due to drying time)

SUPPLIES

For countertop:

- Tape measure
- ¾-inch plywood sized to countertop
- Wood glue and nails
- Wood screws
- Plastic laminate
- Contact cement
- 1x2s cut to fit
- Scalloped decorative fascia strip
- Finishing nails
- Tension rods
- Curtain panels

For ceramic tiles:

- Ceramic floor tiles
- Fine-grade sandpaper
- TSP cleaner
- XIM brand primer
- Oil-based paint: two colors plus white
- Paint tray and liners
- Paintbrushes
- Clean cotton rag
- Water-based polyurethane
- Roller

ROMANTIC-STYLE SURFACES

- **For the countertop base**, join two pieces of ¾-inch plywood with wood glue and nails. Screw to the cabinet base frame.
- **Have plastic laminate cut to fit** at a home center and secure to the plywood countertop with contact cement. Follow manufacturer's directions to apply the contact cement.
- **Edge the countertop** with 1x2s. Add the scalloped decorative fascia with wood glue and finishing nails.
- **For the skirt,** mount a tension rod between frame members above each shelf. Slip curtains with rod pockets over rods.
- **For flooring, add color to plain**, bargain-price white ceramic tiles.
- **Lightly sand tiles**. Clean with a mixture of warm water and TSP cleaner. Rinse; let dry.
- **Apply XIM brand primer**; let dry.
- **Brush on thinned, oil-based paint** and use a rag to remove some of the color; let dry. Two colors, as shown, create an interesting checkerboard effect.
- **Paint the entire tile surface** with a thinned, white, oil-based paint.
- **Allow to dry**. Apply two coats of clear polyurethane following manufacturer's instructions. (Reapply a coat once a year to a clean floor.)

Tip: **Don't drag furniture across the painted tiles**. Never clean with abrasive cleansers. Use a mild liquid cleanser and water, and rinse well.

ROMANTIC-STYLE STORAGE SKILL LEVEL

Advanced

TIME

5 to 6 days
(due to drying time)

SUPPLIES

- Tape measure
- 2x4s cut to size
- 2x2s cut to size
- Wood glue
- Wood screws
- Screws
- ¾-inch plywood shelves, cut to size
- 1x2 cut to fit for fascia board
- Precut ¾-inch, half-round molding
- Finishing nails

ROMANTIC-STYLE STORAGE

Do-it-yourself touches can transform a plain, basic kitchen into an inviting space.

For storage, build simple shelves as an attractive—and economical—alternative to cabinetry.

- **Measure the space and construct a frame** using 2x4s and 2x2s cut to fit, wood glue, and wood screws.
- **Secure the frame to the wall studs with screws** for added stability. Add ¾-inch plywood shelves with a 1x2 fascia board to prevent sagging. (Shelves should span no more than 3 feet without support to prevent sagging.)
- **Secure precut ¾-inch half-round molding** to the front edge with finishing nails.

APARTMENT STYLE

SKILL LEVEL

Intermediate

TIME

4 to 5 days

SUPPLIES

For glazed wall:

- Four colors of latex wall paint
- Glazing liquid
- Roller
- Two roller covers
- Paint tray
- Paintbrushes
- Cotton rags

SUPPLIES

For plate rack:

- 1x4 pine boards cut to size
- ⅜-inch dowels cut to 12-inch lengths
- Hand drill
- Wood glue
- Decorative molding
- Cream or off-white latex paint or your color choice
- Glazing liquid
- Paintbrush
- Cotton rags
- L-brackets

APARTMENT STYLE

- **Glaze worn or plain white walls** with four colors of paint diluted with glazing liquid. Mix in a ratio of three parts glaze to four parts paint for a slightly aged look. Or adjust for the color and coverage you prefer. Allow adequate drying time between coats for a neat, smooth finish.

- **Construct a simple plate rack** from 1x10 pine boards, sized to fit your space, and 12-inch-long, ⅜-inch dowels. Drill holes for dowels with a hand drill and glue dowels between boards with wood glue. Glue on decorative molding. If you prefer an antiqued look, paint or glaze with two or three coats of paint diluted with glazing liquid. Rub off excess paint or glaze with cotton rags.

- **Attach to the wall with L-brackets**.

SOUTHWESTERN STYLE SKILL LEVEL

Intermediate

TIME

1 day (stain only)

SUPPLIES

- Tinted paste wax
- Shoe polish brushes
- Concrete stain (alternative)
- Clean cotton rags
- Spray-on dusting cleaner
- Clean dust mop

SOUTHWESTERN STYLE

This kitchen benefits from touches that enrich its regional style—and the owner's decision to enhance the existing concrete floor.

- **Be bold with color**—especially if you live in a sunny climate. Here, deep violet walls pair with yellow laminate countertops, an inspired if daring choice. A flat paint finish is more compatible with the adobe look of Southwestern style.

- **Add regional decoration**—such as the blue and white Mexican tiles used as the backsplash and baseboard.

- **Introduce aged elements**, such as the tailor's table used as an island and rustic baskets with handles for storage.

- **Update an older concrete floor.** Get professional help for the chemical stripping. (Homes built with slab construction have concrete floors. If you live in a warm climate, consider removing carpeting or other flooring and living with the concrete.) In areas such as the Southwest and Florida, flooring specialty companies have the tools and expertise to stain, refinish, and seal concrete floors. In the kitchen shown, a flooring company stripped off existing paint and chemically etched the concrete floor so that it would accept fresh stain. This is NOT a do-it-yourself project. However, if you would like to finish the project yourself, apply a tinted paste wax with shoe polish brushes, or concrete stain with clean cotton rags. Work quickly; stain dries very fast.

- **To care for a concrete floor**, spray a dusting cleaner on a clean dust mop 24 hours prior to use. Dust-mop the floor, shaking out the mop as it fills with dust, pet hair, and other debris.

QUICK TAKES
SKILL LEVEL
Beginner
TIME
Afternoon
SUPPLIES
- Assorted plates
- Plate hangers
- Level with printed ruler
- Tape measure
- Pencil
- Hammer
- Clothesline wire
- Clothesline hangers
- Clothespins
- Assorted tea towels

QUICK TAKES

Show off a collection and add decorative appeal to your kitchen. Rosy pink plates, alike in style but featuring different seashell motifs, embellish a painted beaded-board backsplash over the sink, *above and top right*. Identical olive-oil cans serve as stylized vases for sprigs of flowers.

- **Be brave with your kitchen color choices**. Lemon yellow pairs with cobalt blue for walls, *right*. The chair rail sports a touch of orange.

- **For an absolutely instant window treatment**, *right,* install a link of metal clothesline as the curtain wire. Secure tea towels to the line with brightly colored plastic-coated clothespins. (If you like a country or cottage look, substitute a twine line, wooden clothespins, and checkered tea towels.) Change towels as the mood strikes or the seasons change.

TABBED SHADE

SKILL LEVEL

Intermediate

TIME

2 to 3 hours

SUPPLIES

- Fusible shade kit
- 2½ yards of 45-inch-wide fabric
- Scissors
- Wooden rod cut to fit
- Fusible tape
- Decorative buttons
- Finials

SPONGED DIAMOND

SKILL LEVEL

Intermediate

TIME

1 day

SUPPLIES

- Fabric
- Kitchen sponge
- Latex paint
- Scissors
- Fray-checking liquid
- Curtain rod and hooks
- 1x4-inch mounting board
- Screws
- Staple gun
- Staples

TABBED ROLLER SHADE

Give your kitchen a tailored accent—and privacy—with this handsome shade. It's surprisingly simple and inexpensive to construct.

- **Start with a fusible shade kit**, purchased at a fabric store. The kits are sold in 42-inch widths and can be cut to fit most windows. Follow directions for fusing the fabric to the shade.
- **For added weight and style**, attach tabs and a wooden rod to the shade bottom. To make the tabs without sewing, cut an 8½ x 5-inch fabric piece. (This example has nine tabs for a 42-inch shade.) Fold the long sides to the center, right sides out, overlapping ½ inch.
- **Insert fusible tape into the overlapped area** and press to secure. Fold under ends ½ inch; secure with tape. Position tabs on fabric shade; hand-sew a button through each tab. Slide a curtain rod through tabs and attach finials.

SPONGED DIAMOND CURTAINS

Dress up your kitchen windows with this cottage-style project. The unhemmed, sawtooth edges make it quick and easy.

- **Sew two panels with rod pockets**, each measuring the window width by length (slightly longer than the sill plus several inches for a rod pocket at the top). Hem the outside edges and stitch the rod pockets. Leave the bottom and inner edges unhemmed.
- **To make the valance**, cut a fabric panel the window width plus 9 inches (for returns) by 28 inches. Fold in half lengthwise, right sides together, and stitch ½-inch seams on short ends. Turn right side out and zigzag-stitch along the unfinished long edge.
- **Cut a kitchen cellulose sponge to 3 inches square.** Start at the center of the valance and stamp diamonds along the bottom (folded) edge. Start in the bottom inside corner of each curtain panel and stamp diamonds along the center and bottom edges. Let dry.
- **Trim excess (unpainted) fabric from the edges of the curtain panels**, leaving a zigzag pattern. (Do not trim the valance edges.) Finish with a fine line of fray-checking liquid, available at fabric stores. Mount curtain rod and hang panels.
- **Screw a 1x4-inch mounting board**, cut to the window width, flush to the top of the window frame so the wide part of the board extends over the curtain. Wrap the top 4 inches of the valance over the board, turning corners gift-wrap style. Staple to secure the valance to the board.

TABLECLOTH TOPPERS

SKILL LEVEL

Beginner

TIME

3 to 4 hours if shade is included

SUPPLIES

- Fusible shade kit
- Hole punch
- Fabric glue or double-sided tape
- Pair of decorative brackets per window
- Wooden dowel per window
- Paint, if wood to be painted
- Vintage or reproduction tablecloth
- Ribbon
- Pins
- Wooden pull rings and narrow ribbon

TABLECLOTH TOPPERS

Enjoy the charm of a vintage or vintage-style tablecloth with this no-sew treatment.

- **Purchase a fusible shade kit from a fabric store**. Follow package directions to fuse fabric.
- **With a hole punch, make a hole near the bottom center of the shade**. Carefully remove the existing shade from the roller blind rod. Attach the custom-made shade using fabric glue or double-sided tape.
- **Install the roller shade to the window frame**.
- **Hang decorative brackets** to support a wooden dowel rod. Drape a tablecloth over the rod and gather it with loops of ribbon pinned at the back.
- **Wrap a wooden pull ring with narrow ribbon**, threading the loose ends of the ribbon through the hole in the bottom of the shade; tie in a bow to finish.

TEA TOWEL SHADES

SKILL LEVEL

Intermediate

TIME

Afternoon

SUPPLIES

- Assorted tea towels
- ½-inch plastic curtain rings
- 1x2 board cut to window width
- ¼-inch wooden dowel cut to width of shade
- Fabric glue
- Staple gun
- Small screw eyes
- Shade-and-blind cord
- Sharp sewing scissors
- Small cleat from hardware store

TEA TOWEL SHADES

■ **Purchase colorful tea towels in colors, styles, and patterns that work with your kitchen.** A fun look, as shown, is to mix colors of the same style towel. To make shades long enough for your window, overlap narrow hems on the short sides of the towels and sew together.

■ **Stitch ½-inch plastic curtain rings to the long hemmed edges of the wrong side of the towels.** Sew the first ring 7 inches from the top of the towel, and the last ring 2 to 5 inches from the bottom hem. Space rings in between every 5 inches, making sure they're even side to side.

■ **For mounting and stability, cut both a 1x2 board and a ¼-inch diameter dowel to the width of the shade.** Slide the dowel through the bottom rings and glue the ends to the towel. Staple the top of the shade to the 2-inch side of the board. On the other 2-inch side, twist small screw eyes in line with each row of rings.

■ **Cut a piece of shade-and-blind cord, purchased from a fabric store, for each row of rings.** Cut one cord double the length of the shade; cut the other cords that length plus width. Determine which side to install the string control and tie the cord to the bottom ring of that side. Tie the longer cords to the other bottom rings. Secure with fabric glue. Run each cord through the rings directly above it and through the screw eyes across the board. All the strings feed through the same eyes. Trim cord ends even and tie together.

■ **For the inside mounting,** staple the 2-inch side of board against the upper window frame; screw carefully in place.

■ **Screw a small cleat from a hardware store** to the side of the window. To raise the shade, pull cords evenly and loop around the cleat.

CONTRIBUTORS/RESOURCES

Pages 8-9,10 Regional editor: Nancy Ingram, Tulsa, OK; photography: Jenifer Jordan, Waxahatchie, TX; architect: Thomas H. Wilson Architectural Design Group, Oklahoma City, OK; contractor: Fab Construction, Oklahoma City, OK; interior design: Fanny Bolen Interiors, Oklahoma City, OK; iron railing and light fixture: Tara Feuerborn, Oklahoma City, OK.

Pages 16-17 Regional editor: Lynn McBride, Charleston, SC; photographer: Cheryl Dalton, Asheville, NC; design: Elizabeth Sullivan, Charleston, SC

Pages 22-23 Styling and photography: Cheryl Dalton, Asheville, NC; architect: John Fisher, Asheville, NC; custom colored tile: Dunis Studio, San Antonio, TX.

Pages 24-25 Regional editor: Mary Baskin, Waco, TX; photographer: Jenifer Jordan; project designer: Charlotte Comer, Dallas, TX; kitchen designer: Delores Key; cabinetmaker: Corkey Burcham; builder: Al Sternennburg; color consultant: Carol Pankratz; color finisher: Sandra Wicham.

Pages 28-29 Regional editor: Nancy Ingram; photography: Jenifer Jordan; designer/builder: Powers Design/Build, Tulsa, OK; kitchen designer: Roger Shollmier, Tulsa, OK.

Pages 30-31 Regional editor: Lynn McBride; photography: Cheryl Dalton; architect: Heidi Brown; cabinetry: Chip Jurgieliwiz; interior design: Jack Patla Antiques, Charleston, SC.

Pages 32-33 Regional editor: Mary Baskin; photography: Jenifer Jordan.

Pages 46-47 Photography: Bill Rothschild, Wesley Hills, NY.

Page 53 Upper left: regional editor: Lynn McBride; photographer: Cheryl Dalton; design: Cynthia Walter Interiors, Edisto Island, SC. lower right: photography: Bill Rothschild

Page 72 Lower left, photography: Bill Rothschild.

Pages 96-97 Regional editor: Andrea Caughey, San Diego, CA; photography: Ed Gohlich, San Diego, CA; design: Sherry Beecher, San Diego, CA.

Pages 98-99 Styling and photography: Cheryl Dalton.

Page 103 Project design and styling: Wade Scherrer, Des Moines, IA; photography: Pete Krumhardt, Des Moines, IA; wainscot and trimwork: Steve Strawn, Des Moines, IA.

U.S. UNITS TO METRIC EQUIVALENTS

To Convert From	Multiply By	To Get
Inches	25.4	Millimeters (mm)
Inches	2.54	Centimeters (cm)
Feet	30.48	Centimeters (cm)
Feet	0.3048	Meters (m)

METRIC UNITS TO U.S. EQUIVALENTS

To Convert From	Multiply By	To Get
Millimeters	0.0394	Inches
Centimeters	0.3937	Inches
Centimeters	0.0328	Feet
Meters	3.2808	Feet